RUBEN DARIO CENTENNIAL STUDIES

RUBEN DARIO

CENTENNIAL STUDIES

Edited by MIGUEL GONZALEZ-GERTH and GEORGE D. SCHADE

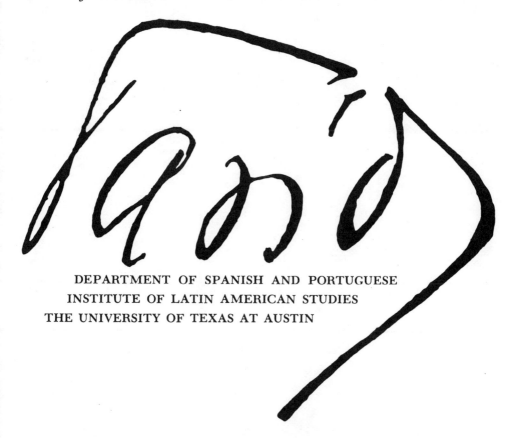

DEPARTMENT OF SPANISH AND PORTUGUESE
INSTITUTE OF LATIN AMERICAN STUDIES
THE UNIVERSITY OF TEXAS AT AUSTIN

FOREWORD

IN FEBRUARY OF 1967 the University of Texas at Austin celebrated the
Rubén Darío Centennial by presenting a series of lectures and other
cultural events organized by the Department of Romance Languages.
The present volume contains the five lectures given on five consecu-
tive afternoons.

The scholars who took part in the symposium represent countries
that played a geographical, intellectual, and sentimental part in the
life of Rubén Darío: Argentina (Anderson-Imbert), Chile (Torres-
Rioseco), Cuba (Florit), Spain (Enguídanos), and the United States
(Phillips). One might say that only France and his native Nicaragua
are missing, unfortunately. Professor Miguel Enguídanos examines
the inner tensions which made Rubén Darío aware of his being one
with the world and comes to the conclusion that, contrary to the postu-
lates of recent times, a lush poem like "Era un aire suave" is not only
characteristic of Darío's sensibility but also as much a work of art as the
broody "Lo fatal"; while at the same time the poet somehow foresaw
the wave of dehumanization which now threatens us. Professor Eugenio Florit points out a number of details in Darío's coming to grips
with the problem of form and shows how the young man who was to
become a lyric star of the first magnitude occasionally foreshadowed
himself in unsure yet interesting compositions. Professor Allen W.
Phillips presents a thoughtful and well-documented study of the
friendly relations and mutual regard that existed between Darío and
Ramón del Valle-Inclán, the great Spanish modernist and expressionist
who cultivated the peculiar kind of literary satire called *esperpento*.
Professor Arturo Torres-Rioseco comments on Darío as a "classic poet"
and contends that what was once regarded as obscurity in his work
actually stemmed from a general lack of culture among many of his
readers, especially since after 1888 (when he published *Azul*) Darío
moved confidently toward an integration of language and emotion
which responded to his preference for classical forms. Lastly, Professor Enrique Anderson-Imbert analyzes what is perhaps the Nicaraguan's most significant literary production next to his poetry, name-
ly, his short stories, among which are many that develop on the plane
of the fantastic. Anderson-Imbert concludes that, although frequently
Darío marred his fiction by relating it to his occultist obsessions, he

sometimes shows himself to have been a master of the prose narrative as well as of the poet's instrument.

It is important to note that the symposium was planned in such a way that the lecturers had complete freedom to choose their own topics and did so independently. Yet the reader will discover, as did we who were there at the time of oral presentation, a surprising unity among the essays. There is a line of vision and feeling that runs from the first to the last, highlighting recurrent themes of great significance, such as the permanent value of poetic art, the relations between the works of a given writer (in this case Darío) and those of his contemporaries, as well as the inner relations among his own works, and the element of foresight in literature or the ancient identification of the poet and the prophet (*vates*).

We wish to thank Professor Ricardo Gullón, who first conceived this centennial celebration and did much to get it under way. For their assistance we should like to express our gratitude to Professor Theodore Andersson, former Chairman of the Department of Romance Languages, to Professor Ramón Martínez-López, Vice-Chairman of the Department of Spanish and Portuguese, and to the members of the organization committee for the celebration: Professors Luis A. Arocena, Michel Dassonville, Beverly J. Gibbs, K. Carter Wheelock, George G. Wing, and particularly to Dr. Nettie Lee Benson, Latin American Collections Librarian, for making accessible many key items from those collections, and Professor Pablo Beltrán de Heredia for planning and executing a splendid book exhibit in the lobby of the Academic Center as well as a very handsome program-brochure. We also wish to convey our special thanks to Mrs. Esther W. Phillips and to four young scholars here at the University, Miss Anne Bonner, Mr. David Flory, Mr. John Wilcox, and Mrs. Cecile Wiseman, for giving so generously of their time to translate the essays included here, and to Dr. Stanley R. Ross, Director of the Institute of Latin American Studies, and his Publications Committee for their assistance in financing the printing of this book. Finally, with the name of Mrs. Julia Reeves, who typed the manuscript, we wish to close these lines of appreciation.

MIGUEL GONZÁLEZ-GERTH

Table of Contents

INTRODUCTION
by George D. Schade

STRADDLING THE NINETEENTH AND
twentieth centuries, Rubén Darío (1867–1916) triumphantly ushers
in the literary movement known in Spanish America and Spain as
Modernism with *Azul* (1888) ('Azure'), a collection of poems and
stories, and *Prosas profanas* (1896) ('Worldly Songs'), a volume of
verse. His pivotal work, however, and the masterpiece of Modernism,
which had such a tremendous impact on Hispanic literature, was
published in 1905, *Cantos de vida y esperanza* ('Songs of Life and
Hope'), a book of poems of such vitality that one feels one has lived
there and shared in its experiences: its gnawing doubts, deep anguish,
and at the same time, quenchless appetite for life. Several other out-
standing collections of verse followed: *El canto errante* (1907) ('The
Errant Song'), and *Poema del Otoño* (1910) ('Autumn Poem'), which
contain individual pieces that haunt the memory and fire the imagination. In addition to his poetry, Darío produced a large corpus of prose
work: some fine short stories ranging from the jeweled anecdotes of
Azul to splendid Gothic tales of suspense and horror; critical notes on
and often flamboyant appreciations of contemporary writers, *Los raros*
(1893) ('The Odd Ones'); a rather slap-dash but charming autobiography; travel impressions, *España contemporánea* (1901), etc.

Confronted by his work on this centennial anniversary of Darío's
birth, the critics have been busy trying to assess once again his place in
Hispanic letters. During his lifetime Darío enjoyed enormous re-
nown, but in the half-century since his death, the poet's star has
plummeted in the minds of some: a writer garlanded and anointed
during his brief years on earth, then duly interred in the Histories of
Literature and Anthologies of Hispanic Poetry, jettisoned in favor of
more modern voices often of harsher, bleaker tones. Undeniably, some
of these poets, like Pablo Neruda and Octavio Paz, who follow Darío
in Spanish America, are towering geniuses, but to prefer their poetry
should not automatically make one scorn Darío's.

Rubén Darío was born in a humble hamlet in Nicaragua. At the
age of fifteen he began his nomadic wanderings, visiting neighboring
El Salvador; at nineteen he embarked for Chile where he spent several
crucial years in his literary development and published his first sig-

nificant book of poetry. Later he lived for fairly extended periods in
Argentina, Spain and France, and in these three countries produced
the bulk of his best creative work: compelling poems of enduring
beauty, style and dignity. During his short and active life Darío undoubtedly suffered a great deal, but he also drew in deep, hearty
breaths of life. At times he plumbed abysses of alcoholic dissipation,
but his poetry soared heaven-ward in a constant endeavor to attain
spiritual beauty. Now his home and haunts (in Nicaragua, in Spain,
etc.) have become places of pilgrimages, and his lasting fame seems
assured.

All attempts to gloss over Darío's genius by churlish critics are
doomed to failure. If we select from the best of his work, not only
Cantos de vida y esperanza, but also *Prosas profanas*, *El canto errante*
and *Poema del otoño*, the truth of this genius emerges clearly. His
poetry has substance and surface, a supporting wall as well as the
brilliant stucco façade. *Prosas profanas* delight our senses with their
rich tapestry of recurring exotic and mythological patterns. They are
like pictures with finish and glaze. This richness and refinement of
phrase is combined seductively with an unerring sense of rhythm and
music to enchant our ears as well as feast our eyes.

The perfection of form continues in *Cantos de vida y esperanza*.
Darío, the master craftsman, the distiller of exotic essences and per-
fumes extracted from many lands and arts, does not falter. But his
earlier tendency toward rhetoric and ornamentation often gives way
here to melancholy poems full of shadows and blendings, self-probings
and doubts, the hermetic seclusion of the inner world, the anguish
which characterizes so much of twentieth century literature. Death
becomes more apparent thematically; it is a part of life and until it is
accepted, life is perhaps but a subterfuge.

In several poems of *El canto errante* a very modern note is struck
where Darío startles us by employing deliberately common, conversa-
tional phrases, which are so conventional in present-day poetry, but
atypical of Darío. His hedonistic "Autumn Poem" again represents
Darío at his best—magnificent verses pulsing with the heartbeat of
life.

Unprecedented and unmatched in the annals of Spanish American
literature, Darío's poetry fertilized a whole generation, and his influence continues to be felt. On re-reading his poems, we find that they
give pleasure and stimulate reflection; we discover more beauty, more
meaning in them.

The Department of Romance Languages of the University of Texas celebrated his centenary in February, 1967, with a week of symposia, exhibitions of his books, and lectures by distinguished scholars on various aspects of Darío's work. These lectures are published here in English translation in the hopes that the English-reading public in this country and Great Britain, in recent years more aware of Hispanic letters, will find them provocative and interesting, and perhaps be stimulated to read Darío himself.

A work may be many things at the same time, but it is important to know what the essential things are in it. The quarries our authors seek in the following pages are some of these essential things in Darío's poetry and prose. We offer them as a tribute to his memory.

2

Cuando el aureo Pegaso
En la victoria matinal se lanza
Con el mágico ritmo de su paso
Hacia la vida y hacia la esperanza,
Si alza la crin y las narices hincha
Y sobre las montañas pone el casco sonoro
Y ~~hacia la~~ hacia la mar relincha,
Y el espacio se llena
De una gran temblor de oro,
Es que ha visto desnuda a Anadiomena.

Gloria, oh Potente. a quien las ~~sombras~~ temen!
~~Gloria ti~~
Que las más blancas tórtolas te inmolen..!
Pues por ti la floresta está en el polen
Y el pensamiento en el sagrado semen!

Gloria ~~a esto~~ oh Sublime que eres la existencia,
~~Que ...~~ en quien siempre hay futuro en el útero eterno,
~~...~~ tu boca sabe al fruto del arbol de la Ciencia
Y al torcer tus cabellos apagaste el infierno.

[Fragment of Darío's autograph of *Carne, Celeste Carne.*]

MIGUEL ENGUÍDANOS

INNER TENSIONS IN THE WORK OF RUBÉN DARÍO

translated by Cecile Wiseman

So MUCH HAS BEEN WRITTEN about the work of Rubén Darío that I have to be cautious. Anyone who wants to say something new about his work is immediately confronted by a formidable obstacle: not only is his critical bibliography already very extensive, since he is considered the Spanish-American poet par excellence, but also some of these studies are of very high quality. Pedro Salinas' book, *La poesía de Rubén Darío,* stands out among the very best. I will confess at once that for me this book has been as much guide and inspiration as obsession and nightmare. To say something more, something that will penetrate deeper into Rubén's work than what Salinas has already said, is, frankly, very difficult.

Salinas combined his great critical talent and his exceptional humanity and personality, with an even rarer gift—he was himself a true poet. Thus he could penetrate the subtleties of the poetry of Jorge Manrique and Rubén Darío from multiple personal perspectives: that of the poet, that of the critic and professor, that of the emigrated Spanish liberal—never free from his Spain, but in love too with this new world—and that of the whole man, the well-bred man of good taste.

Salinas' book about Darío is the child of an epoch. Its essential concern is with themes: to find the true themes of the poetry. It is concerned as well with style: how and why the themes are expressed as they are. But although Salinas' work is a difficult mark to surpass, and even though read with the respect that such an admirable effort deserves, it presents still only one point of view. Subtle and penetrating, but not final. No one human point of view is absolute. At the end of his book Salinas, with his usual integrity, recognizes and points out this limitation. He covered a great deal of territory, but nevertheless he himself, in his conclusion, points us toward the areas still unexplored in Darío's vast work. His methodology not only admitted other possible approximations, but also suggested the direction that other kinds of studies could follow. I could not have written these pages if

I had not read this challenging message in the last lines of Salinas' book. He says:

Thus I see the themes of Darío's poetry—the central and the minor ones— not as drawn by my judgment or prejudice, but as evident and completely objective facts in his poetic reality. Three active principles, *anguished eroticism* (the inevitable intertwining of the acts of creation and death), *social concern*, and the idea of *art and the poet*, function in his poetry, perfectly distinct, each one seemingly enclosed in its own orbit. In the realm of objective reality they are undoubtedly completely independent. But fate brought them to live together in the poetic creation of Rubén. Is it possible for these three great themes to have coincided in his spirit, merely dwelling in the same shelter, keeping themselves apart and separate without any form of fecund contact or enriching communication? It is unquestionable that the themes do not touch at any point, if they are considered one by one, *abstractly*. But they have one thing in common: independent among themselves, the three are still dependent upon the same master, the spirit of the poet. . . . The themes don't touch each other, but do all three touch the same soul?

Clearly Salinas understood that considering Darío's work as a jig-saw puzzle—and the image is his, not mine—into which all the fundamental pieces had to be fitted before the ultimate and final image was revealed, left one task still undone. In his own words, it was still necessary "to discover the latent capacity for coherence among them," among the fundamental pieces. Salinas, then, did not over-look the need for carrying the search for understanding to what I have proposed as one of the chapters of my work: to determine how the poet lived his visions in anguished inner conflict.

Proclaiming anguished eroticism as one of Darío's themes, Salinas saw the necessity for going even further:

Anguished eroticism kept Darío in a *state of constant war with himself*. The two antagonists into which his nature was split hardly gave him an instant of rest—moments of exalted and jubilant unconsciousness, truces that divided the acts of his drawn-out tragedy. The poet felt his spirit possessed by the terrible truth that *struggle* is the inescapable fate of any erotic desire that wants to endure. This gave birth to a *growing longing for peace*. . . . This *tragedy of the poet* began, as we know, the first day of battle between the erotic and the temporal, between Eros and Chronos.

The "constant state of war," or the "tragedy," in which the poet lived, a supremely erotic-melancholic consciousness, is something that readers. These tensions are, in short, the energy that maintains the particles of his being in cohesion. To use another technological metaphor, they are his electric charge; true poetry, then, will be charged with a kind of radioactivity. Which explains the burns it inflicts upon those of us who come genuinely close to it. What I have said about my last working hypothesis is true for all great poets, especially for the modern ones, and in especially great measure for Rubén Darío. In the fine inner tensions of his poetry lies the ultimate secret of his work.

My methodology in this task obliges me to examine the poet's work at length. (I intend to make all the necessary explorations gradually. These observations are part of a book on the work of Darío which I am currently writing. However, the working hypotheses outlined above apply to the entire book and not merely to the present chapter.) At this point it is better for me to be very selective and reserve until later my faithfulness to the order of the poet's vital experiences. I too must be careful and watch out for pitfalls, and, at best, establish some poetic-existential coordinates in Darío's work that will let me test the validity of my hypotheses.

Darío's biographers have established the important facts of his everyday life. They aren't hard to enumerate or understand; I will mention a few that are related to his precocious infancy and adolescence.

Rubén was born in a remote and insignificant corner of the Hispanic world. His town was poor, his family was poor—not only in material things but even more in spiritual means. His childhood was dominated by the stigma of abandonment, separation from his parents, sadness and insecurity. Some claim that the child Rubén found himself surrounded by gossip that cast doubt upon his paternity. He was brought up by a great-aunt and uncle, good people but eccentric. His uncle and godfather was a colonel in a small country, a fervent liberal who held degrees in law and philosophy, a disorderly reader. He treated him like a true father, but, to add misfortune to misfortune, he died when Rubén was still a child. The lack of a real home was compensated for by the boy's precocious development. Among his various precocities— political, erotic, alcoholic—his gift for verse was apparent very early. It is said that when he was eight years old he was already known as the "child-poet." Early in his adolescence he became famous as a local poet. His international consecration, we must remember, came with the publication of *Azul* . . ., when he was twenty-one. In other words, he found rapid recognition in the craft for which he seemed pre-

destined. To balance accounts in everything else his life was an un-
broken chain of failures and personal misfortunes. He was never free
from insecurity, or even from extreme hardship in facing the vicissi-
tudes of everyday life.

But all this is important only because the constants of loneliness,
bitterness, and misfortune are present in Rubén's poetry, from his
first stumbling efforts to his greatest and most enduring poems. It
can be said, obviously, that there have been other lives as unhappy as
Darío's, and unfortunately there will be many more, and that—as
Salinas said—the relation between the innumerable events that the
poet lives as a simple human being and the exceptional acts that are
his poems has still to be proven. Although I realize the difficulty of the
problem that Salinas poses, I refuse to separate those exceptional facts
of life, the poems, from the existential context in which they are produced. This affirmation, which I find myself repeating over and over,
is at the point of becoming a downright platitude; but I believe my
insistence is necessary, because what I ask of my readers is a simple
act of vital commitment to poetry. An act so simple, and so obvious,
that its necessity can be overlooked. What I ask is nothing more than
to insert the poems into the chain of insignificant events, and consider
them higher events, that is, to see them and feel them like events of
life that are culminating and revelatory of the whole chain. Neither
biography nor psychology is to be feared, if the scholar's perspective,
like that of the reader, is directed from the poem toward life, and not
from life toward the poem. In the poems, I insist once more, we find
the true life of the poet.

This poem, one of Rubén's earliest—written when he was fourteen
—and of little literary value, is worth considering:

> Lector: si oyes los rumores
> de la ignorada arpa mía,
> oirás ecos de dolores;
> mas sabe que tengo flores
> también, de dulce alegría.

> (Reader: if you hear the faint sounds
> of my unknown harp,
> you will hear echoes of pain;
> but know that I have flowers
> too, of sweet joy.)

The little poem (intended to appear on the title-page of a proposed first book) is composed mimetically of obvious resonances and literary allusions—the harp, the echoes of pains, the flowers of sweet joy. It is not at all noteworthy or exceptional. The lines would have been forgotten and never recovered if they had not been Rubén's. The poet himself dismissed them, not wanting them to be published. Alberto Ghiraldo, Darío's heirs, and the scholars have salvaged them. And they do in fact serve a purpose.

The purpose they serve for me is to point up the fact that at this early stage the boy-poet, even though derivatively, was already speaking of some "faint sounds," some songs, charged with inner tension. The conflict is very simple, but conflict nevertheless: "If you hear the faint sounds . . . you will hear echoes of pain; *but* . . . I have flowers *too*, of sweet joy." The vertices of tension are clearly established, the charge and irradiation of that anguish is not very effective, but its direction couldn't be clearer: to make us hear the faint sounds of the harp, the inner, unknown music that speaks to us of the contradiction between pain and joy. Perhaps the literary model for this early exercise was Bécquer or one of the other Romantic poets, but the intention, the desire, to tell us that life is made up of pains and joys, is it only a literary cliché, not really felt, or is it already a true intuition of what awaited the poet?

All this would be gratuitous or irrelevant if there weren't a line of continuity that could be traced from that little poem of 1881 to the great poems, like the autobiographical one that opens *Cantos de vida y esperanza*: the constant presence of that first tension. And even more: Rubén tells us in that poem, as he looks back on his first years:

> Yo supe de dolor desde mi infancia;
> mi juventud. . . ¿fue juventud la mía?
> sus rosas aún me dejan su fragancia,
> una fragancia de melancolía. . .
>
> (I have known pain since childhood;
> my youth . . . was it really youth?
> its roses still lend me their fragrance,
> a fragrance of melancholy. . .)

The examples are very numerous and should be studied in detail, their chronology established, and the variations and modifications, as well as the outcome, of the pain-pleasure vertices traced.

I am going to proceed selectively in order to test the viability of some of my hypotheses. I will consider two examples that not only seem to me highly significant, but are without doubt two of Darío's best poems. They are "Era un aire suave . . . ," written about 1893, the first poem of *Prosas profanas*, and "Lo fatal," the last poem of the book *Cantos de vida y esperanza*, written before 1905.

I begin with "Lo fatal" for a particular reason. Today, as yesterday, the reader makes his own anthology of Darío's works. He excludes poems and prose that he considers to be of transitory merit, fashionable in their time but no longer saying anything today. This is natural. In his recreative task the reader searches for that part of the poet's work that has not only resisted the attacks of time, but that he feels to be closest to his own sensibility. It is necessary to consider how much the fashion of the selector's era will influence his choice. It is possible that many times synchronization with the contemporary weighs more than the desire to find permanent poetic merit.

"Lo fatal," without question, is a great poem; but, at the same time, it has become the classic example of composition by Darío that we cite unblinkingly, saying that "this is the part of Rubén's work that deserves to be saved." I wonder if the fact that today many of Darío's readers would consider "Lo fatal" worth saving, but might relegate to oblivion "Era un aire suave . . . ," does not have more to do with the "fashion," or preferences of today's reader, than with the true value of the poem.

Consider "Lo fatal":

> Dichoso el árbol que es apenas sensitivo,
> y más la piedra dura, porque ésta ya no siente,
> pues no hay dolor más grande que el dolor de ser vivo,
> ni mayor pesadumbre que la vida consciente.
>
> Ser, y no saber nada, y ser sin rumbo cierto,
> y el temor de haber sido y un futuro terror. . .
> Y el espanto seguro de estar mañana muerto,
> y sufrir por la vida y por la sombra y por
>
> lo que no conocemos y apenas sospechamos,
> y la carne que tienta con sus frescos racimos,
> y la tumba que aguarda con sus fúnebres ramos,
> ¡y no saber adónde vamos,
> ni de dónde venimos. . . !
>
> (How fortunate the tree, almost without feeling,
> and even more the hard rock, because it feels nothing now,
> for there is no greater pain than the pain of being alive,
> nor heavier burden than conscious life.

To be, and to know nothing, and to be without a sure direction,
and the fear of having been and a future terror. . .
and the certain dread of being dead tomorrow,
and to suffer from life and from shadow and from
what we don't know and scarcely suspect,

and the flesh that tempts with its fresh-clustered fruits
and the grave that awaits with its funeral wreaths,
and not to know where we are going,
nor from where we have come. . . !)

Read today, this seems to us one of Rubén's most profound poems. What it communicates—its feeling that pain and absurdity are the dominant notes of human existence—has disquieting resonances for us.

How many times, as we leaf through the paper in the morning and read articles that tell us of social, economic, political, and now cosmic absurdities, and others that detail the ins and outs of the latest atrocity, how many times don't we feel exactly the same mood expressed by the poet? Today it is a group of respectable citizens that questions very seriously the human dignity of people who have a higher proportion of melanin in their skin. One morning we hear that someone is defoliating an entire jungle, with great efficiency, of course, burning out the trees, the animals, and the people who lived there. We can suppose, like the poet, that the rocks at least felt nothing. Another day we read that the dangers of cigarette smoking have been proven, to find, on the next line, a statistic showing that in view of this fact, the number of smokers has increased. Another morning we're told of prodigious machines that go to the moon and to Mars, take pictures of these mysterious heavenly bodies, send the pictures to Earth, and publish them: we look at them and see—that there is nothing there. We hear too, every day, about the politics of brinkmanship.

The poet had anticipated our sensibility back in 1905: ". . . to suffer from life and from shadow . . . and not to know where we are going, nor from where we have come . . . !" "Lo fatal" is unquestionably a good poem. But it is also true that we read it today, and prefer it to others, because it expresses so exactly what we feel inside of us, giving voice to the anguish of our time.

At the beginning of the century Rubén had already felt and expressed modern man's existential anguish and sense of loss. He was seeing the advance—in fact he had already expressed it bitterly in the stories of *Azul . .* in 1888!—of the frightening dehumanization that followed from the subordination of the spiritual to the material;

the subordination of man to the thing, the artefact. "Lo fatal" is the naked expression of pure existential tension. The polar vertices of the tensions are perfectly clear in the poem:

Mineral and vegetable existences—rock and tree, in order of vitality —opposed to human existence—conscious life, feeling.

Being—with a consciousness or inclination for knowledge—opposed to "knowing nothing."

To feel the passing of time, opposed to a refusal to accept condemnation to temporality.

The fear of having lived before and forgotten—it is known that Rubén was a spiritualist—opposed to the terror of returning to live another earthly existence.

The tempting flesh, demanding the erotic act of creation, opposed to the grave, of funereal flowers.

The unknown origin of man, opposed to his uncertain final destiny.

These are the constant vertices of tension, successive or alternating, of human existence. Rubén feels them and lives them in the poem, stripping his soul naked before us with an almost absolute candor and intensity. He bares for us the very heart and bowels of his poetry. He hasn't dressed up this poem with the irritating, glittering, or ultra-sonorous draperies that we have come to expect. Almost all that remain are the rhythm of the lines, unmistakeable and always masterly, and two sensual metaphors: "frescos racimos" ("fresh-clustered fruits") and "fúnebres ramos" ("funeral wreaths"). The poem's stylistic charge is in the verbs: *to be* (several times), *to know* (also various times), *feel, be dead, suffer, suspect, tempt, wait, go, come*; all of them in repetitive play, being conjugated in different tenses. The nouns too: *life* (twice), *pain* (twice), *tree, rock, burden, direction, fear, terror, dread, shadow, flesh, fruits* ("racimos"), *grave, wreaths*. Notice that the simple enumeration of the poem's verbs and nouns almost gives us the experience of the entire composition; although, naturally, we know syntax to be especially important in this poem. One construction in particular stands out, being repeated thirteen times in a poem of thirteen lines: the accumulation of terms joined by the copulative conjunction "and." It is this repetitive construction, accumulating tensions, that communicates to us the pain and fears of the poet, and that produces the great discharge of existential agony.

Rubén Darío himself, in his *Historia de mis libros* (1909), explained his intentions in their vital and historical aspect:

In "Lo fatal," against my deep-rooted religion, and despite myself, a phantasm of desolation and doubt rises like a fearful shadow. Certainly, there has existed in me, from the beginning of my life, a profound pre-occupation with the end of existence. . . . I have been filled with anguish when I examined the basis of my beliefs and discovered my faith to be neither solid nor well-founded enough when conflicting ideas have made me waver, and I have felt myself lacking a constant and firm support. I have known the cruelty and idiocies of men. I have been betrayed, repaid with ingratitude, slandered, misinterpreted in my best intentions by the evil-minded, attacked, vilified. And I have smiled sadly . . .

It would not be difficult to select and study other poems by Rubén like "Lo fatal," where the poet, human and profound, smiles *sadly* at men's idiocies, or tells us of the anxieties that trouble his heart. I mention only "¡Ay, triste del que un día. . . . !," "Augurios," "Melancolía," "Thanatos," from *Cantos de vida y esperanza*, "¡Eheu!" from *El canto errante*, "Poema del otoño," from the book of the same name, and the poems "A Francisca." There are many more of this kind. Consider, for example, "De otoño," also from *Cantos de vida y esperanza*, a key poem for the understanding of the poet's reversion and his concentration on the inner song, where he says:

> Pasó ya el tiempo de la juvenil sonrisa:
> ¡dejad al huracán mover mi corazón!

> (The time of the youthful smile has passed:
> let the hurricane move my heart!)

Or the spine-tingling "Nocturno," poem XXXII of *Cantos de vida y esperanza*, of maximum importance in understanding how the tension of the poet's soul turns the dial of his poetry:

> Y el pesar de no ser lo que yo hubiera sido,
> la pérdida del reino que estaba para mí,
> el pensar que un instante pude no haber nacido,
> ¡y el sueño que es mi vida desde que yo nací!

> (And the regret of not being what I would have been,
> the loss of the kingdom that was meant for me,
> the thought that for an instant I could have not been,
> and the dream that is my life since I came to be!)

What I have said is perhaps not new. The group of poems to which I have referred is, as I pointed out earlier, the part of Rubén's work that the readers of our time would salvage from a shipwreck. The rest, especially the most characteristic poems of *Prosas profanas*, don't awaken much interest; they are considered—when they are paid any attention at all—as exquisite frivolities, or as porcelain museum pieces. Today few readers would jump into the water to save the work of "the other" Rubén Darío.

"Era un aire suave . . . ," from *Prosas profanas*, is a poem that moves hardly anyone today, and that, at best only scholars and specialists in Spanish-American literature read with any interest. Nevertheless, I think that we are committing a great error of historical perspective and aesthetic appreciation. As I said earlier, the judgments fashionable in our age are suppressing real efforts to understand and feel the enduring merits of that poetry.

To begin with, I find highly doubtful—and a grave historiographic error—the dichotomy made between the Rubén of before and the Rubén of after *Cantos de vida y esperanza*. Those who believe in this dichotomy have not asked themselves whether a creative existence is not perhaps a biological and historical continuity. The reality that is a succession of physio-biological moments in the poet's life has a corresponding parallel, even more complex and rich, in the succession of moments in the self-formative process and in the creative process. In order to know the life of a man, what a man really is, we have to know his history. Among the innumerable events that happen during his existence, the ones that make him *him*, the ones that shape him, are his most individual, original, and creative acts. We, the majority of human beings, don't get far along this road, and, at most, our formation culminates in the acquisition of a unique personality and a collection of abilities. But there is a minority, made up of the original thinkers, the inventors, the artists, the poets, who possess the gift of making, of shaping, not only their personal history, but also that of the majority. They bring about great and transcendent events. How can we understand a poet's life, or the guts of his life that is his work, if we mutilate it, or even worse, if we don't make an effort to relive it on its own terms?

Rubén Darío's whole life passed in incessant movement. Always in tension, because, disliking the succession of nights and days that it was his lot to live, he tried to cast off these contingencies and direct his soul, and his work, toward an ideal world; a world more like a utopia, metamorphic and changeable, than an ivory tower. The great adventure that was his life, despite sorrow and misfortune, can be under-

stood and justified only by reading, really reading, *all* his poetry. The
study of his anecdotal biography should be subsidiary to that of the
flow of his work. The sufferings of one who knew himself to be
defenseless, not at all pragmatic, a Chorotega Indian, who went
stumbling through life, matter to us because, as he was careful to tell
us, he had the hands—creative hands—of a marquis. His aristocratic
dreams reflect more the exaltation of the human spirit than an aspiring
social vanity. His aristocratic and exquisite ways, acquired with great
effort, were part of being a poet. They are a pathetic adventure, ended
happily only in his work, and they caused Rubén more pain than joy.
He indulged in certain worldly vanities during his term as minister of
Nicaragua in the court of Alfonso XIII, or during his trips through the
Hispanic world, where he had become an idol; but they were all very
precarious. The uniforms and palaces were only lent, backdrop to a
farce in which he himself never really believed. His poetry—more
than the documents and chronicles of the period—tell us the whole
truth.

Tying all the loose ends, I read "Era un aire suave . . ." Yes. The
poem seems to be, at first sight, the dream of an ideal, exquisite world.
The music comes up and a female character appears: the marquise
Eulalia, a literary fiction who embodies literature, dreams, a vision of
the eternal feminine—"laughter and fickleness" ("risas y desvíos")—
and an illusion of an aristocratic and supercivilized world. Lavish
aestheticism. Verses and lines that would irritate other poets—among
them Unamuno—because taken out of context, they were acoustic
pyrotechnics. Remember the most famous verse, the one that provoked
the wrath of the harsh and austere don Miguel:

> ¡Amoroso pájaro que trinos exhala
> bajo el ala a veces ocultando el pico;
> que desdenes rudos lanza bajo el ala,
> bajo el ala aleve del leve abanico!

> (Amorous bird that breathes out trills
> under her wing sometimes hiding her beak;
> that hurls forth coarse disdain under her wing,
> under the treacherous wing of the light fan!)

But if we read the poem ("Era un aire suave . . .") with care and
awareness of those inner springs that stretch from the poet toward
every horizon, until the creative and unifying tension is produced,
we will notice that the gentle airs heard in the gardens and salons of

the palace, the laughter of the marquise, her coquetries, are heard
and contemplated from a distance, from outside the gratings that
separate the garden, and its fortunate inhabitants, from the common-
ers. There, banished, in his condition as the humblest of men, is the
poet. In the poem the marquise Eulalia surrenders herself to the page-
servant-poet; but she does it in the garden, hiding herself from those
of her class in "el boscaje que cubre la amable glorieta" (the foliage
that covers the inviting bower). Afterwards the exquisite Eulalia keeps
on laughing and flirting; the party goes on . . .

When we get to the last five lines, we realize that it has all been a
dream. The poet doesn't know where or when he saw the marquise,
nor when he heard her laughter. The time and space in which it all
took place was only an illusion. The dream's effect is cruel, the poet
is hurt:

> ¿Fue acaso en el Norte o en el Mediodía?
> Yo el tiempo y el día y el país ignoro;
> pero sé que Eulalia ríe todavía,
> ¡y es cruel y eterna su risa de oro!

> (Was it perhaps in the north or in the south?
> I know neither the time nor the day nor the country;
> but I know that Eulalia is laughing still,
> and her golden laughter is cruel and eternal!)

The laughter hurts the dreamer, naturally, because he knows that
he is excluded from the dream. That is the poem's real inner tension,
its secret. The poem is not an exquisite porcelain museum piece, but a
sad song of the longing to possess that porcelain. The frivolous laugh
of the marquise never ends: "Eulalia ríe todavía." Rubén hears it
always there within, in the dream-salon that he can never enter in
prosaic reality.

Obviously there are differences between the Rubén of *Cantos de
vida y esperanza* (1905) and the Rubén of *Prosas profanas* (1896).
The poetic ingredients, the magnitude of the different inner tensions,
can vary from one period to another, and this variation will be evident
in the final product, the individual poems; but the differences are the
logical result of living in time—a process always painful for Rubén,
and the Gordian knot of his poetry. They will be seen with greater or
lesser clarity, but a good reader will always find the poem's extremes
of tension and its emotional trajectory.

A letter written by Rubén in 1904 to his loyal friend Juan Ramón

Jiménez, when he was preparing and selecting the *Cantos*, is quite enlightening in this respect. Rubén says, among other things:

I am going to send you the poems very soon [those intended for the volume *Cantos de vida y esperanza*]. You'll see. There's a little of everything. But for the first time there is what Rodó didn't find in *Prosas profanas*, the man who feels. It must be that when I wrote them, *although I was suffering* [italics mine], I was in my springtime and that consoled me and gave me courage and joy.

Our current injustice to the so-called first Rubén, then, shouldn't surprise us. If writers who were really so close to him, like Rodó and Unamuno, didn't see the underlying suffering and gentle melancholy in his springtime verses, how can we expect it of ourselves, here in another age—atomic and apocalyptic?

Today it is difficult to relive Rubén Darío's imaginary adventure of marquises, Versaillesque gardens, princesses, and swans. We prefer to say that they died away, thank God, his visions ended forever. Eager for the simplistic formula—and wanting to pass quickly over something that no longer charms or intrigues us—we reduce it all to the statement that the poetry of gentle breezes, lyres, gardens, and marquises, was a fashion that fulfilled its function in a given moment—the end of the nineteenth century and the beginning of the twentieth—by battling against the ugliness, prosaism, and vulgarity prevalent then. But by simplifying so drastically, we deny ourselves the understanding of the high tension with which these poetic visions were charged—and still are charged—for the reader. We refuse to feel with Rubén the spiritual tension, the inner shock—beyond all changes of fashion—that drove him to dream his deliriums or chant his hymns, to find an outlet for his tremendous verbal and imaginative exuberance. We don't sympathize with this poetry because in us the organ for feeling it and enjoying it has surely atrophied. It is possible, too, that we have come to the extreme of being incapable of seeing the hunger for higher beauty and humanity that can be felt by a man born in the lowest, darkest, and remotest roots of a village, rich in sensibility but poor in fortune, justice, and happiness.

Rubén Darío was born in Metapa, an insignificant spot; all his life he walked in a dream of lakes and distant palaces. But it would be unjust to call him an escapist for this. He became a cultured man, in his own way, a way that was partly that of the Hispanic world, that is, improvised, autodidactic. He lived concerned with the great and small things that happened around him. He felt himself committed to many causes and ideas of his day. He was a modern man—more than a Modernist—and he knew as few did, in those years at the end of the century, that a flood of dehumanizing dangers was coming upon us. In a curious parallel with Unamuno, Rubén undertook a humanizing mission. He already knew, in those years, that the idea of satisfying only the material needs of the villages was inadequate. He, who had known every kind of privation, knew very well that the hunger of the poor is not "hunger" in the singular, but "hungers," in a resounding and demanding plural. Hunger for human dignity; hunger for mastery over nature, things, time, and distance; hunger and thirst for justice; hunger for beauty, cleanliness and health; and above all, the hunger of hungers, that of the spirit.

Rubén realized that a great historical era, one given direction by successive aristocracies, was coming to an end in his time. He saw on its way a violent flood of Prussian artillerymen, of pragmatic Yankees, of English stockbrokers; he didn't foresee the coming of the super-bureaucrats, especially the Bolsheviks. He thought the flood inevitable, but he feared, with reason, that something worth saving would be lost in it. Something superfluous, without apparent social function, not even edible; something that couldn't be used to build the modern anthills intended for the perfection of mankind. Something that Rubén, timid, always somewhat of a child, progressively deeper in alcoholism, useless for everything but writing, symbolized, saw, sang, questioned, grieved, in a swan.

Rubén's swans weren't —aren't—papier-maché decorations, contrivances of Wagnerian stage machinery. They were chaste and noble heraldic symbols, pennants of challenge, and much more. Improbable animals that seem artificial to us today, forgotten in lakes and rivers by the poets of other times. Anachronistic, even a little vulgar, if you wish; but they're there still. . . . Bad readers of Rubén that we are, we haven't realized that the poet put more expressive force in his persistent use of the word "still" than in the laughter of the marquise Eulalia or in the whiteness of the swans.

Although in remote times swans had been the dream of minstrels, or the emblem of knights (Cisneros), they had come to be only a part of the closed garden of the few. Rubén, from the critical vantage point of his lifetime, asked them, the few, not to forget the last song, nor why the swan sings it. The many, those who were going to tear down forever the gratings of the world's Versailles, he asked not to strangle the swans, to learn the lesson of art and mystery hidden in their form. Once more the old myth could be life-giving. The swan must not be strangled. He must be saved, fed, left tranquil and majestic in his lakes, to see if the old humanizing gods, taking form once more in him, would come down to earth to impregnate new Ledas: seamstresses, typists, working girls, free now from servitude to the land or to rich masters, but about to fall into the dehumanizing trap of the factory, the office, the union, and the party. The swan could do something to combat the mediocrity of the middle class Ledas that today, a hundred years after Rubén's birth, is already in possession of the world. Bread for everyone! by all means, but why not swans too? thought with hope and pain the good Indian of Chocoyos.

Today, a hundred years after he was born, we think about the poet and are saddened as we contemplate the spectacle of these masses of whites, reds, blacks, yellows, and greens that can conceive of no other bird than the chicken bred on an industrialized farm, and that prefer the racket of parades at Macy's, in New York, or in Moscow's Red Square, to the tranquility of the lakes.

The following words come from a letter sent by Rubén Darío to the Cuban writer Manuel Serafín Pichardo, on August 21, 1907:

One of the things I most appreciate in you, my good friend, is your loyalty to the purity of Art in the midst of life's ugliness. There are so many toads and so few swans!

In this simple lamentation directed to a friend and poet, in the intimate language of a letter, we can see resumed the maximum inner tension that moved Rubén. He knew himself to be physically, socially, and practically closer to the toad than to the swan. The tension between the ugliness of life and the purity of Art mattered to him more as that tension in itself—a striving toward human fulfillment—than as an aesthetic posture. He praised his friend's decision to dedicate himself to lofty humanizing ideals: the toads are so many, but the swans so few! If there is so much toad in each of us, why not dream, why not strive to become a swan?

RUBEN DARÍO

———

AZUL...

I. CUENTOS EN PROSA
II. EL AÑO LÍRICO

VALPARAISO
IMPRENTA Y LITOGRAFIA EXCELSIOR
14, CALLE SERRANO, 14
—
MDCCCLXXXVIII

EUGENIO FLORIT

THE MODERNIST PREFIGUREMENT IN THE EARLY WORK OF RUBÉN DARÍO

translated by John Wilcox

IN THE FOLLOWING PAGES, I PROPOSE to convey some of the ideas that occurred to me as I read the poetry that Rubén Darío wrote prior to *Azul*. Obviously, for such a task I have had to lean on certain studies that have already been done on the subject, and also on certain opinions expressed, even though in passing, by distinguished colleagues and critics.

In the first place, the poet's precociousness and his truly prolific output have to be borne in mind. His early work begins around 1878, when he was hardly eleven years old, and goes on to 1888, the date of the first edition of *Azul*. If we include in this production all the verse Darío wrote up to that year,[1] we find ourselves dealing with almost half, and perhaps more than half, of the total number of his poetic compositions. In them, as is natural in an exceptional case such as this, we do observe from the outset stutterings, approximations, or prefigurements of what his poetical language was destined to become within a very few years. My dear friend, Enrique Anderson-Imbert, among others, has already indicated in his excellent introduction to Ernesto Mejía Sánchez's edition of the poems, how Rubén Darío, before his journey to Chile and when he was still in his native Central America, had begun to feel the influence of French writers of the time: Coppée, Mendès, Gautier. His initiation into the harmonious groves of Victor Hugo, thanks to his friend Francisco Gavidia, should be included here.[2] It is clear, says Anderson-Imbert, that before his journey to Chile he sympathized with Parnassian ideals of "art for art's sake," "but even after having glimpsed the course he would have to take, he went round and round like a distracted dove that circles the city, delaying the moment at which he must part to deliver his message."[3]

It is some of these wanderings that I would like to mention, even if they do no more than mark a few of the milestones on his trajectory. I hope that the reader will discover with me Rubén Darío's struggle, as I like to call it, with form; a form in pursuit of which he was end-lessly engaged. Let us recall the final poem of *Prosas profanas*:

YO PERSIGO UNA FORMA . . .

Yo persigo una forma que no encuentra mi estilo,
botón de pensamiento que busca ser la rosa;
se anuncia con un beso que en mis labios se posa
al abrazo imposible de la Venus de Milo.

Adornan verdes palmas el blanco peristilo;
los astros me han predicho la visión de la Diosa;
y en mi alma reposa la luz, como reposa
el ave de la luna sobre un lago tranquilo.

Y no hallo sino la palabra que huye,
la iniciación melódica que de la flauta fluye
y la barca del sueño que en el espacio boga;

y bajo la ventana de mi Bella-Durmiente,
el sollozo continuo del chorro de la fuente
y el cuello del gran cisne blanco que me interroga.[4]

In addition, there are some curious points to be found by those who wish to steep themselves in Darío's relations with poets who were older or younger than he. The admiration and enthusiasm that the name of Rubén Darío awoke in the young Juan Ramón Jiménez is known to all. I say 'the name' because Juan Ramón himself has said and written on different occasions that, when he saw Darío for the first time in April of 1900, he had read few of his poems. Graciela Palau de Nemes states that, in spite of Juan Ramón's admiration, his verse shows the influence of Rubén Darío only after he had met the great Modernist bard in person.[5] Is it, then, just coincidence, mere chance, an influence absorbed through contact with the poetical milieu? There is one certain piece of evidence: among the poems Rubén Darío wrote in his adolescence, there is one in *romance* verse-form[6] entitled "La niña de ojos azules" ('The Blue-eyed Girl'). Al-though the poem has no date, Méndez Plancarte places it with those written between 1882 and 1884. The poem is divided into three parts. It has an assonance in "i-a," is similar to a madrigal and is sentimental in tone. The third of these parts opens with these four lines:

Cuando la hablé de mi amor
inclinó la frente tímida;
y como perlas, dos lágrimas
rodaron por sus mejillas.[7]

> y parece que murmuran
> algo de las hojas secas
> y de las flores difuntas.[12]

Undoubtedly, this is a foretaste of some of the early Juan Ramón *romances*, found in his "Rimas de sombra" ('Rhymes from the Shade') and *Arias tristes* ('Sad Arias').

As far as José Martí is concerned, Max Henríquez Ureña says in his *Breve historia del Modernismo*: "The influence of Martí, to whom Darío devoted several articles of remarkable criticism, beginning with the one that appears in *Los raros*, is already seeping through to aspects of his prose style. In 1891 Martí published *Versos sencillos*, and some of the turns of phrase and lyrical tendencies of these poems found an echo in later compositions of Rubén Darío. For instance, in his "Elogio a Don Vicente Navas" (1893), Darío models verses that imitate Martí's 'manner,' as Regino Boti has remarked."[13] Indeed, Boti, the Cuban poet and critic, has managed to isolate some of the lines or verses in Rubén Darío that are very close to the Martí of *Versos sencillos*.[14] He highlights these *redondillas*:[15]

ELOGIO A DON VICENTE NAVAS

> Tejo mi corona, llévola
> para honrar al ciudadano
> que hubiera puesto su mano
> sobre las brasas de Escévola. . . . ;
> a quien, por firme y leal,
> el deber bronce daría;
> a quien el alma tenía
> fundida en bronce moral.
>
> Loor, pues, a quien fue noble,
> honrado, viril, sin tacha
> El leñador movió el hacha;
> cayó el varón como un roble.[16]

In this instance, it can be clearly seen that Darío had read not only Martí's prose, about which so many good studies have been done, but also his poetry. Nevertheless, it happens that if we examine the work done by Rubén Darío prior to 1891, the date of publication of the already mentioned *Versos sencillos*, we discover many instances reminiscent of Martí's octosyllabic combinations. In fact, I have a special interest in these "instances." They first attracted my attention in 1962. Indeed, I did, in passing, point them out at that time in my study

Juan Ramón, in a poem entitled "Adolescencia" ('Adolesc
the following:

> No se atrevía a mirarme;
> le dije que éramos novios,
> ... y sus lágrimas rodaron
> de sus ojos melancólicos.[8]

Is it not a fact that there exists a real resemblance of tone an
vocabulary? "Two tears rolled" in the first of the poems,
tears rolled" in the second. Both feminine figures are timi
girls. But what emerges as something out of the ordinary i
yet still surrounded with pleonastic padding, is already wel
lished in Juan Ramón, and the poet, in our opinion, is maste
word and tone. Credit for this is due in part to the selective
used in the preparation of the Hispanic Society's edition of
escojidas ('Selected poems').[9] The editor had the good taste to
nate those poems of inferior quality which appear in Juan Ra
first two books, *Almas de violeta* ('Souls of Violet') and *N*
('Water Lilies') (1900). But, I insist that it is curious how both
separated by a distance of twenty years, somehow end up off
each other a handshake that was wet with the tears of a girl in
youth. There also exists another example of a similar close re
blance in Darío's *Romance*, which for some unknown reason is
cluded from Méndez Plancarte's edition:

> Era una tarde de enero;
> el sol casi se ocultaba,
> y las brisas dulcemente
> gemían entre las ramas... [10]

Another *romance*, the second of the poems in *Rimas* ('Rhymes'
(1887), may also serve to point out those echoes of Rubén Darío i
Juan Ramón Jiménez. It begins this way:

> Amada, la noche llega;
> las ramas que se columpian
> hablan de las hojas secas
> y de las flores difuntas.[11]

And it ends in this exquisite manner:

> En tanto los aires vuelan
> y los aromas ondulan;
> se inclinan las ramas trémulas

of Martí's verse.[17] I believe that the first example of *redondilla* octo-syllables to be found in the Cuban poet's work is the delightful poem "Dormida" ('Asleep') (1878), which, however, was not published until many years after Martí's death, and therefore could not have been known by Darío in 1880. After this, we have to wait until 1889 when he writes "Los zapaticos de rosa" ('The Little Pink Shoes') for his review, *La Edad de Oro*. Then we have the whole gamut of various octosyllabic combinations in *Versos sencillos*. As far as Rubén Darío is concerned, the *redondillas* appear even in his first collection, to which the poet himself gave the title "Sollozos del laúd" ('Sobs from the Lute'), but which never appeared in print as such. There is, for example, the poem "Desengaño" ('Disillusion'), probably written in June 1880, some of whose verses are more than adequate to illustrate this point. He writes:

> De la fuente las espumas
> se miraban blanquear,
> y en los espacios cruzar
> pájaros de airosas plumas.[18]

A poem that does resemble Martí, though unwittingly, such as the one entitled "Cámara obscura" ('Dark Chamber'), should be situated chronologically, as don Alfonso Méndez Plancarte has done, in or around 1882. We should read it all, because within these verses we shall find the characteristic style, that particular vein of *Versos sencillos*. It reads as follows:

> La calle de la Amargura
> nos ve llevar nuestra cruz;
> pero en la cámara obscura
> penetra un rayo de luz.
>
> En la mía, no da el cielo
> un solo rayo feliz;
> la mía tiene un tapiz
> de fúnebre terciopelo.
>
> Tiene la tuya del día
> el espléndido irradiar;
> de la noche el sollozar
> es lo que tiene la mía.
>
> Bajo mi cámara obscura
> Cristo gime en un madero;

> bajo ella, un sepulturero
> cava una honda sepultura.
>
> Bajo la tuya, su historia
> pintó el ángel del trabajo;
> y las coronas que trajo
> muestra el ángel de la gloria.
>
> Neurótico y visionario
> gózome yo en tu labor:
> cuando vas a tu Tabor,
> voy subiendo mi calvario.
>
> Ve cómo es la suerte rara:
> juntas dicha y desventura;
> la tuya, cámara clara;
> la mía, cámara obscura.[10]

This poem, especially the first stanza, the third and fourth lines of the second, and the whole of the fourth, has the very rhythm, the very manner, the same characteristics, the same spirit of Martí's *Versos sencillos*. Yet another example: "El organillo" ('The Little Organ'), of 1881, which belongs to the series of poems dedicated to the Central American patriot, Máximo Jerez. Here are three quatrains:

> Busca y pide; la doblez
> recoge por lo que quiere:
> al fin, Máximo Jerez
> deja el organillo y muere.
>
> . . .
>
> Sí, otro anciano marcha ahora
> con el organillo; ha de ir,
> camino del porvenir,
> por la calle de la aurora.
>
> Y el viejo y pobre instrumento
> de la canción de la Unión
> ha de poner su canción
> sobre las alas del viento.[20]

Another example is found in "A unos ojos" ('To a Girl's Eyes') (1884) of which the first verse reads:

> El sol con sus rayos rojos
> ya no brilla, ya no arde;

que está dormida la tarde
y está dormida en tus ojos.[21]

In another poem, of about the same year, which is entitled 'Introducción a "La Aurora" de Joaquín Méndez' ('Introduction to "The Dawn" by Joaquín Méndez'), we read

. . . color rosado en las nubes
que se mecen con donaire,
ruidos de alas en el aire,
como que vuelan querubes;

en redes de flores, presos,
gorriones y mariposas,
y los lirios y las rosas
como si se dieran besos;

estremecimientos vagos
en las hojas y en las brisas;
por todas partes sonrisas,
aquí un eco, allí un halago;

el césped, de olor cubierto,
junto al riachuelo sonoro,
y un ave con pluma de oro
sobre un capullo entreabierto;

una bella que camina
junto a un joven trovador;
él le habla cosas de amor,
y ella la cabeza inclina;

y mientras el aire deslíe
recio, tenue y liviano,
él la toma de la mano,
y ella le mira y sonríe.[22]

Another Martí 'instance' appears in 1888, "La lira de las siete cuerdas" ('The Seven Stringed Lyre'), written by Darío in January of that year in Santiago de Chile for Elisa Balmaceda y Toro's album. The poem is divided in seven parts or 'strings'. Each part has a different structure; the length of the lines and of the stanzas varies. It is only the first part that is of interest to us:

¿Cantar a la dama? Bien
está, por belleza y fama,

y es muy justo que a la dama
galanterías se den.

¿Cantar a la niña? Es cosa
que más mi lira prefiere.
Soy un loco que se muere
por los botones de rosa.

Tú, ni dama ni niña eres,
porque estás en el divino
crepúsculo matutino
en que nacen las mujeres.

Luz y gloria son tus galas,
ángel eres y en Dios sueñas:
tú debes tener las señas
donde tuviste las alas.[23]

This brings us up to the prologue of *Abrojos* ('Thorns') (1887)
which is written in *redondillas*. The book is dedicated to Manuel Rodríguez Mendoza to whom this initial poem is addressed. It contains
verses of a similar tone to those already mentioned. Here are a few
random examples:

Juntos hemos visto el mal
y, en el mundano bullicio,
cómo para cada vicio
se eleva un arco triunfal.

. . .

Vimos perlas en el lodo,
burla y baldón a destajo,
el delito por debajo
y la hipocresía en todo.

. . .

Mucho tigre carnicero,
bien enguantadas las uñas,
y muchísimas garduñas
con máscaras de cordero.

. . .

La envidia que desenrosca
su cuerpo y muerde con maña;
y en la tela de la araña
a cada paso la mosca. . .[24]

Had Martí read any of these verses? It is possible only if they were published in reviews, or if the Cuban poet possessed a copy of *Abrojos* or of *Rimas*. But let the patient scholar answer such questions, for I neither am nor claim to be one. Rather, while reading these poems, so valuable in themselves, I have been interested only in noting that resemblance of tone, of expression, of vocabulary, and even the voluntary repetition of interior rhymes, as in the case of the composition written for the album of Elisa Balmaceda y Toro. They present us with a Rubén Darío who, around the year 1882, when Martí was publishing his famous free hendecasyllables, was already writing such extraordinary poems as one we have recently quoted, "Cámara obscura." This poem is a direct antecedent, although Darío did not know it, of what Martí himself was going to say eleven years later.

As we are dealing with relations and antecedents, I should like in a quick parenthesis to refer to a case of 'echo-ism' which I have found in one of Rubén's famous poems, and in one by José Eusebio Caro. In this case, I believe there is no doubt that the poet from Nicaragua read the poet from Colombia. Caro's verses were published in 1885 in Madrid, and "Canción de otoño en primavera" ('Song of Autumn in Springtime'), dedicated to Gregorio Martínez Sierra, appeared in *Cantos de vida y esperanza* ('Songs of Life and Hope') in 1905, when Rubén himself was living in Madrid. It is rather interesting to note the form of both poems: quatrains with lines of nine syllables, ending with consonant rhyme, masculine in the odd-numbered ones. Darío's poem is longer: seventeen quatrains and a final line of either eight or nine syllables, depending on how you make the synalephas. Caro's poem has ten stanzas. In place of the melancholy sensualism of the first, there is a tone of serenity and a predominance of nostalgia in the second. In "Estar contigo" ('To Be With You'), Caro writes:

> ¡Oh! ¡ya de orgullo estoy cansado,
> ya estoy cansado de razón;
> déjame en fin, hable a tu lado
> cual habla sólo el corazón!

> ¡No te hablaré de grandes cosas;
> quiero más bien verte y callar,
> no contar las horas odiosas,
> y reír oyéndote hablar!

> Quiero una vez estar contigo,
> cual Dios el alma te formó;

tratarte cual a un viejo amigo
que en nuestra infancia nos amó;

volver a mi vida pasada,
olvidar todo lo que sé,
extasiarme en una nada,
¡y llorar sin saber por qué!

The last line reminds us of Rubén's line "a veces lloro sin querer" ("at times I weep without wanting to"). The poem continues:

¡Ah! ¡para amar Dios hizo al hombre!
¿Quién un hado no da feliz
por esos instantes sin nombre
de la vida del infeliz,

cuando, con la larga desgracia
de amar, doblado su poder,
toda su alma ardiendo sacia
en el alma de una mujer?

¡Oh padre Adán! ¡Qué error tan triste
cometió en ti la humanidad,
cuando a la dicha preferiste
de la ciencia la vanidad!

¿Qué es lo que dicha aquí se llama
sino no conocer temor,
y con la Eva que se ama,
vivir de ignorancia y de amor?

¡Ay! ¡mas con todo así nos pasa;
con la Patria y la juventud,
con nuestro hogar y antigua casa,
con la inocencia y la virtud!

Mientras tenemos despreciamos,
sentimos después de perder;
¡y entonces aquel bien lloramos
que se fué para no volver![25]

This final line is parallel to Darío's "te fuiste para no volver" ("you left, never to return") and its variant that is more often repeated "¡ya te vas para no volver!" ("you leave, never to return"). Is it not a fact, that in meter, accentuation, rhyme and even in that refrain, Rubén's song persistently brings to mind Caro's, or vice versa? This is just another curious point that I bring forward, in case nobody has noticed it before.

Now, I shall discuss something that I consider to be more important. I tried to find among Rubén Darío's initial poetical output some lines, verses or 'moments' in which the poet strides ahead of himself. That is to say, when his poetical language seems to be cutting a path for itself from among all the jaded foliage of useless verse. I expressed this once in a sort of aphorism: "How much useless verse before getting to the poetry, if one ever can get there!" Obviously, Rubén did; but arduously, by wrestling against his innate facility to versify, and against that essential impatience with living that led him along so many and such varied paths, until he eventually found his real self. Julio Saavedra Molina in his article on Rubén Darío's first book, *Epístolas y poemas* ('Epistles and Poems') or *Primeras notas* ('First Notes'), sketches a guideline which will help us glimpse what really interests us. He says: "As is to be expected, there are also in *Epístolas y poemas* of Managua (1885)—or rather, as Méndez Plancarte has observed: the *Primeras notas* of the false cover of 1888, —some foreshadowings that are rather typically Rubén Darío, —I mean, some heralding of what this poet's Modernism will later be."[26] He also quotes an example which we shall stop to examine later. But let us continue at a measured pace to examine the texts in the order in which they appear in Méndez Plancarte's edition. It is my opinion that this is a good edition to follow because it is complete and well arranged. However, I take exception to some of the titles that are given to different sections prior to *Epístolas y poemas* and after *Canto a la Argentina y otros poemas* ('Song to the Argentine and Other Poems') (1914). Such titles as "Iniciación melódica" ('Melodic Initiation') and "Del chorro de la fuente" ('From the Fount's Flow'), borrowed by the compiler from the final sonnet of *Prosas profanas*, strike me as rather unnatural, because they are taken out of context. With all due respect to Méndez Plancarte, I prefer the previously used titles:[27] "Poemas de adolescencia" ('Adolescent Poems'), "Poemas de juventud" ('Poems of Youth') and "Lira póstuma" ('Posthumous Lyre'). It is a pity that more care was not taken to arrange the chronological order of the poems grouped under these titles. In Méndez Plancarte's edition, on the other hand, the order has been carefully determined.

In the first place, we must remember, as Ernesto Mejía Sánchez says in his study of the classic humanities in Rubén Darío,[28] that from

an early age our poet mentions the names of Greek and Latin writers
and mythological characters that he had acquired through reading.
He never ceased to draw on classical antiquity and to treat it in his
poems. At times, we find, of course, that this antiquity has apparently
been transformed by his knowledge of French poets. ("More than the
Greece of the Greeks, I love the Greece of France," he says in *Prosas
profanas*.) This fondness comes to him very early, as does his interest
in civic and political matters. Such themes fill his first work, and they
reappear in some of his most powerful poems in *Cantos de vida y
esperanza*. On the other hand, there is his taste for the sumptuous and
the decorative, which makes its triumphal entry with the "Serenata"
('Serenade') of 1882. This poem opens with a series of fourteen-
syllable quatrains with masculine rhymes (or *rime riche*) in the
alternate lines. These are the alexandrines that he surely worked on
while in the company of Francisco Gavidia:

> Señora: allá en la tierra del sándalo y la goma,
> bajo el hermoso cielo de Arabia la Oriental,
> do bullen embriagantes la mirra y el aroma,
> y lucen sus colores la perla y el coral. . . .[29]

The dodecasyllabic line, comprising two units of seven and five syllables respectively,[30] in rhyming couplets makes its appearance in
1886. In "Cantilena", a ballad, the poet begins with some rather bad
quintillas[31] and then suddenly changes the form of the verse. He is
certainly inspired as, injecting impulse, rhythm and cadence into the
lines, he exclaims:

> Virgen ardiente y pura de Nicaragua,
> tierna como la silfa reina del agua:
> de tus labios de rosa mana ambrosía,
> y de tus negros ojos, la luz del día.[32]

Here is the artist who is master of his palette. A little later on he writes:

> allí, en tus negros ojos irresistibles,
> he comprendido cosas incomprensibles;
> el fuego de tu mente que te ilumina,
> algo es como un destello de luz divina;
> y en el fondo de tu alma de soñadora,
> luce, en fuego apacible, plácida aurora.[33]

Among these poems written between 1882 and 1886, among the commonplace themes and long stretches of verse that say nothing, there

are to be found many drops of honey that gradually grow in size. This is what happens with some of the hendecasyllabic lines of "El poeta y las musas" ('The Poet to the Muses'). The following comes from his first book of poems, *Epístolas y poemas:*

> Batió el Pegaso el ala voladora,
> irguió la crin, y del Olimpo heleno
> hirió la cumbre con el leve casco;
> y el poeta preludió su hosanna eterno.
>
> El padre Apolo derramó su gracia,
> el padre Apolo del talento regio,
> aquel del verso rítmico y sonante
> que llenaba el abismo de los cielos.[34]

The poet is now twenty years old, and he is already familiar with the rhythms of poetry. However, time must pass before he will direct the flight of his Pegasus, even though the magnificent alexandrines of "Víctor Hugo y la tumba" ('Victor Hugo and the Tomb') are already apparent. These alexandrines are certainly prolix, perhaps too prolix, but they contain some first-class verses, such as these:

> Soplaron los tritones su caracol marino;
> las sirenas, veladas en un tul argentino,
> a flor de agua entonaron una vaga canción,
> y se unieron al coro de las ondas sonantes;
> y el mar tenía entonces convulsiones gigantes
> y latidos profundos como de corazón.[35]

This is the verse form and the meter of the "Sonatina," though in major key. In "Ecce Homo," a long poem with philosophical tendencies, there suddenly appears this exclamation:

> ¡Ah, los astros, los astros!
> ¡Ah, carbunclos y perlas y alabastros!
> ¡Infinito joyel; grandiosa altura. . . .[36]

an exclamation that springs with transcendental impetus like a cross or fountain from the middle of a rather mediocre, prosaic and vulgar poem.

In 1889, in San Salvador, he composed a "rhymed chronicle," entitled "Tres horas en el cielo" ('Three Hours in Heaven') about a school function. It is deliberately prosaic in nature, not lacking in wit. At one stage in a conversation he has with a friend, he points out one of the ladies at the gathering and says about her:

> Sí; la que tiene sus cabellos de oro
> como espigas mojadas por la lluvia.[37]

Once again there is poetry in the simplest and briefest of words. And a little further on there is suddenly a "flow" of purest lyricism in a most astounding expression:

> Entró una turba de lirios,
> una insurrección de rosas,
> un gran batallón de hermosas
> y un diluvio de delirios.[38]

Just like that! Then, the "chronicle" continues, and nothing else occurs; only that *redondilla* which, nobody can deny, is a real gem. However, there is this which appears a little earlier in the same poem:

> Abilia Flores, niña süave,
> lanzó una ráfaga de melodía,
> cual si muriendo cantara un ave
> cuando desmaya la luz del día.[39]

A year later, there is "Laetitia," a hymn to happiness which ends with two splendid lines that are so distinctly Darío:

> y se enciende la vida de la tierra
> con la llama invisible del amor.[40]

There are also these two isolated hendecasyllables of "A una estrella" ('To A Star') which recall his lines to "Venus," of which they seem to be the prelude:

> Princesa del divino imperio azul,
> ¡quién besara tus labios luminosos! . . .[41]

And the beautiful "Lied" (whose date Méndez Plancarte suggests is possibly 1890):

> Mirad ¡qué delicia! . . .
> La aurora triunfal,
> su pelo de oro
> y el cesto de rosas que riega en la tierra y el mar.
>
> ¡Y luego, una estrella
> y el rayo de luz
> por donde camina, volando a la estrella que adora
> un pájaro azul!

To this we could add the eighth poem of "El salmo de la pluma" ('The Pen's Psalm'), which is supposed to have been written between 1888 and 1889, and which, in my opinion, is a magnificent prefigurement of his "Responso a Verlaine":

> Pan vive; nunca ha muerto. Las selvas primitivas
> dan cañas a sus manos velludas, siempre activas
>   siempre llenas de ardor.
> ¿Dónde no se oye mágico su armónico instrumento,
> del árbol regocijo, delectación del viento,
>   delicia de la flor?[42]

I said 'prefigurement' because throughout this composition Darío uses a six-line stanza. Structurally, there are two rhyming alexandrine couplets, each followed by a line of six syllables. In his "Responso a Verlaine," he uses the same type of structure. The six-syllable lines are, admittedly, replaced by nine-syllable ones, but they, like the short lines of the "Salmo," end with an oxytonic rhyme.

In the same way, the Versailles described in "Era un aire suave . . ." is already prefigured, although in a different form, in the first sonnet of a series of four entitled "La revolución francesa" ('The French Revolution'). These were written in San Salvador on the fourteenth of July, 1889. Here are two parts from the first sonnet; the first quatrain:

> De raso azul vestidas están las bellas damas,
> Entre tapices llenos de asuntos de Watteau;
> la reina danza alegre, sus ojos son dos llamas;
> habrá lirios como ella, pero más blancos, no.

And the first tercet:

> Gentil el paso mide, su cuello real erguido,
> sonriente y desdeñosa su linda boca en flor;
> paloma de alabastro que tiene de oro el nido . . .[43]

Let that suffice.

We can already see how Rubén Darío's lyrical spirit was gradually trained in these exercises. The last samples are, admittedly, taken from work later than the first edition of *Azul*, but they might easily have been included in that book without discrediting the other poems. I have not been able to resist the temptation to transcribe them. Why? Because they are so little known and because they contain so much of what is purely poetic in Rubén Darío, he who was able to pursue with speed and without respite the ascent of the luminous ladder of poetry.

NOTES

[1] See the latest editions of his complete poems published by Aguilar: *Rubén Darío: Obras poéticas completas,* ed. Federico Sainz de Robles (Madrid, 1945); *Rubén Darío: Poesías completas,* ed. Alfonso Méndez Plancarte (Madrid, 1961); all references in this article are to the 1961 edition by Méndez Plancarte (hereinafter called P.C.) unless otherwise stated.

[2] See E. Anderson-Imbert, "Voluntad de Innovación en Rubén Darío," *La Nación,* (Buenos Aires, March 4, 1951), and *Rubén Darío; Poesía,* ed. Ernesto Mejía Sánchez, Fondo de Cultura Económica (Mexico, 1952).

[3] Mejía Sánchez, *Ibid.,* p. xi.

[4] P.C., p. 699.

[5] *Vida y Obra de Juan Ramón Jiménez* (Madrid, 1957).

[6] Octosyllabic verse with second and fourth lines in assonance.

[7] P.C., p. 168.

[8] Juan Ramón Jiménez: *Pájinas Escojidas,* ed. Ricardo Gullón, Editorial Gredos (Madrid, 1958), p. 21. This book has been translated into English by Eloïse Roach and published by the University of Texas Press (Austin, 1962).

[9] New York, 1917.

[10] Sainz de Robles, *op. cit.,* p. 59.

[11] P.C., pp. 561–562.

[12] *Ibid.,* p. 562.

[13] Quoted by Max Henríquez Ureña, *Breve historia del Modernismo,* Mexico, 1962, p. 94.

[14] See "Martí en Darío", in *Cuba Contemporánea,* January 1925.

[15] Eight-syllable quatrain with rhyme abba or abab.

[16] P.C., pp. 1071–1072.

[17] *José Martí, Versos* (New York, 1962).

[18] P.C., p. 8.

[19] *Ibid.,* pp. 17–18.

[20] *Ibid.,* p. 69.

[21] *Ibid.,* p. 176.

[22] *Ibid.,* pp. 195–196.

[23] *Ibid.,* p. 99.

[24] *Ibid.,* pp. 512–513.

[25] *Poesías,* Madrid, 1885.

[26] Santiago de Chile, 1938.

[27] See the Sainz de Robles' edition of *Obras poéticas completas* (Madrid: 1945).

[28] "Las humanidades de Rubén Darío. Años de aprendizaje", in *Libro Jubilar de Alfonso Reyes* (Mexico, 1956).

[29] P.C., p. 123.

[30] In Spanish: *dodecasílabo de seguidilla.*

[31] A stanza composed of five eight-syllable lines and employing two rhymes.

[32] P.C., p. 137.

[33] *Ibid.,* p. 138.

[34] *Ibid.,* p. 374.

[35] *Ibid.,* p. 439.

[36] *Ibid.*, p. 447.
[37] *Ibid.*, p. 1036.
[38] *Ibid.*, p. 1039.
[39] *Ibid.*
[40] *Ibid.*, p. 1044.
[41] *Ibid.*, p. 1045.
[42] *Ibid.*, p. 1024.
[43] *Ibid.*, p. 1028.

Director artístico : LEO MERELO ✤ Administradores : ALFRED & ARMAND GUID

MUNDIAL
MAGAZINE

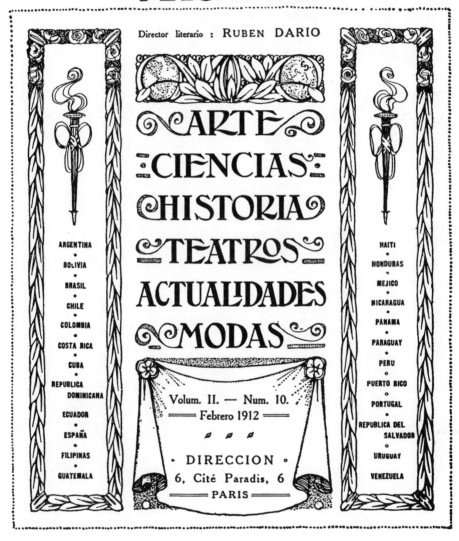

Director literario : RUBEN DARIO

ARTE
CIENCIAS
HISTORIA
TEATROS
ACTUALIDADES
MODAS

ARGENTINA
•
BOLIVIA
•
BRASIL
•
CHILE
•
COLOMBIA
•
COSTA RICA
•
CUBA
•
REPUBLICA DOMINICANA
•
ECUADOR
•
ESPAÑA
•
FILIPINAS
•
GUATEMALA

HAITI
•
HONDURAS
•
MEJICO
•
NICARAGUA
•
PANAMA
•
PARAGUAY
•
PERU
•
PUERTO RICO
•
PORTUGAL
•
REPUBLICA DEL SALVADOR
•
URUGUAY
•
VENEZUELA

Volum. II. — Num. 10.
═══ Febrero 1912 ═══

✍ ✍ ✍

• DIRECCION •
6, Cité Paradis, 6
═══ PARIS ═══

[Sample cover of the review edited in Paris by Darío.]

ALLEN W. PHILLIPS

RUBÉN DARÍO AND VALLE-INCLÁN: THE STORY OF A LITERARY FRIENDSHIP

translated by Esther W. Phillips

ON THE OCCASION OF THE DOUBLE centenary of Rubén Darío and Valle-Inclán, we propose in this study to offer a few considerations about the firm friendship, literary and personal, which existed between the two writers from the moment of their first meetings in Spain in 1899 to 1914, when Darío left for America on his last and final journey. Up to now, whatever has been said about this deep friendship, well known to everyone, does not go beyond generalities, and we hope therefore to indicate here, with greater exactitude and on the basis of appropriate documentation, the extent of their mutual admiration, manifest, as we shall see later, in many forms.*

* After this lecture had been translated, I received further information concerning the literary friendship between Darío and Valle-Inclán. Antonio Odriozola kindly sent me his article "Una desconocida dedicatoria de Valle-Inclán a Rubén Darío," published in *ABC*, July 11, 1967, reproducing the inscription borne by the second edition of *Sonata de estío* (Madrid, 1906). The inscription, later deleted, reads as follows: "A Rubén Darío: con toda mi admiración y mi amistad." Odriozola points out that this was Valle's way of reciprocating since the Nicaraguan had sent him from Paris his "Soneto autumnal al Marqués de Bradomín," which appeared as frontispiece to the second edition of *Sonata de otoño* (1905).

More important, though almost unknown, are some lines written by Darío apparently between 1899 and 1900, in which he refers to his Spanish friend. There is no doubt that they precede the well-known commentary entitled "Algunas notas sobre Valle Inclán" and yet, in them, Darío not only recreates Valle's personality but also reveals interesting insights about the novel esthetic prose-style of works such as *Epitalamio* (". . . a precious little book [*librito bijou*] whose only blemish might be the excessive emulation of Gabriele D'Annunzio and its exaggeration of the delicate") and *Femeninas* ("This is the first instance in which over a correctly written Spanish narrative passes the shadow of French birds in flight"). The text also includes allusions to two other works then in progress: *Tierra caliente* ("reminiscences of travels in [Spanish] America") and *Adega*, in the first chapters of which, already published in journals, Darío finds ". . . the same mannered qualities, the same concerns with plasticity and rhythm, the recognizable devices and the artfulness of D'Annunzio." These lines have been published by Dionisio Gamallo Fierros in *Revista de Occidente*, IV, 44–45 (Nov.–Dec. 1966), pp. 362–363.

Closely united by their devotion to art and by the same aesthetic preoccupations, Darío and Valle are both essentially creators of an individual style. It is true that the Spanish writer came relatively late to literature and that he elaborated part of his early work under the obvious influence of the renovation wrought by Modernism. Soon and progressively, however, he withdrew from a style really foreign to him, passing beyond the aristocratic exquisiteness inherited from Darío and other models of the epoch, to forge his own manner, the style of the later *esperpentos*, which belong to his last and most characteristic period. And it is precisely writers like Unamuno, Juan Ramón Jiménez and Alfonso Reyes who recognize Valle-Inclán's linguistic creativeness. To say that he begins a part of his work with a clearly modernist imprint is not to deny the great originality of his talent, apparent in his first books and carried thence, incorporated with new qualities, into an art that is personal and modernist at the same time. In spite of this filial tie, Valle later departed from the modernist inheritance, as far as outer manifestation is concerned, to enter the regional, time-honored territory of his own tradition. We are well aware of the difficulty of synthesizing adequately the aesthetic trajectory of a writer as complex as Valle-Inclán. Only as an approximation is the habitual formula valid: from *modernismo* to *esperpentismo*. Or this other: from impressionism to expressionism. That is to say, an evolution which starts from an aristocratic aesthetic and the exquisite preciosity of a literature finding inspiration more in art than in life (the *Sonatas*), to reach later on a more transcendent human expression, less gratuitous and less frivolous (the *esperpentos*). Keeping strictly to these two simplifying formulas would mean passing over significant intermediate stages: the pastoral *Flor de santidad* (1904) and *Aromas de leyenda* (1907); the stage of the first *Comedias bárbaras* (*Aguila de blasón* 1907, *Romance de lobos* 1908); that of the three historical novels of the Carlist cycle whose main interest lies in their being an antecedent of those of *Ruedo ibérico*; and lastly certain stories of varying dates, related either to his legendary and mystical style or to the more violent and barbaric one. Nor should we forget new excursions into a scene, still modernist and Versaillesque, in *Cuento de abril* (1909) and *La marquesa Rosalinda* (1913). This last is a transitional work which, with its burlesque tone, anticipates the new attitudes that are to appear very clearly in 1919 with the publication of *La pipa de kif*, a book which is, in turn, an unmistakable forerunner of Valle's modes of expression and thematic preoccupation in his final period. On the other hand there are those who see the work of the Spanish writer as merely a progressive *esperpentización* of reality, discerning from an earlier time scattered elements which will later coagulate and take first place in the genre of the *esperpentos*.

However, through the years and despite many changes in his work, Valle-Inclán always remains true to his profound literary friendship with Darío, who died precisely at the moment when the course of his Spanish friend's writing was about to change. We should like to bring up here a testimony which proves the continuing respect and admiration that Valle felt for the American poet. Angel Lázaro remembers how he and Rivas Cherif used to accompany Valle back to his house in the early hours of the morning. When asked if he still admired Darío in spite of poetic evolution from Modernism to the present, he answered:[1]

Rubén Darío is our great lyric poet. Before him we had none, none in our language. We had, yes, great dramatic poets in Calderón and Lope; but a lyric poet of this dimension, a lyric poet like Petrarch or Dante, this we did not have until Rubén Darío appeared with his great orchestration. Darío—he said it himself—is the complete lyre.

Let us now go on to observe the beginnings of this intimate personal and literary friendship.

Meetings: testimony and anecdotes

Rubén Darío arrived in Spain for the second time on the first of January 1899, commissioned by *La Nación* of Buenos Aires to comment in his chronicles, later collected in the volume *España contemporánea* (1901), on the situation of the country directly after the national disaster of 1898. Let us think for a moment about the date of his arrival in the Peninsula. The triumph of Modernism had been consolidated: Darío himself had published three brilliant books and American youth had rallied to him almost unconditionally. He was, then, at that moment, a consecrated figure of the new literature, and his supremacy was soon acknowledged by the Spanish writers who, in their turn and in their own way, were only a little later to revolutionize Peninsular letters.

Another great friend of Darío and Valle, Juan Ramón Jiménez, who it might be said in passing has written some of the most penetrating pages known about the American master, remembers the time of Darío's second residence in Spain in this way:[2]

But Rubén Darío, synthesis of all this new French poetry, loved Spain like a child, and came to Spain loaded with what he could give her: poetry . . . Rubén Darío lives on in Madrid with the same rank of journalist as Martí, his predecessor on *La Nación* and in Spain; a new Martí, another in love with Spain, in revolt body and soul against injustice. Rubén Darío was considered friend and master by a part of the generation of '98, influenced as they were by some of *los raros*, by Rubén Darío and other rare souls: Ibsen, Nietzsche, Maeterlinck . . . Jacinto Benevente, then chief of the renascence, admired him frankly; Ramón del Valle-Inclán read him, re-read him, quoted and then copied him; others including cognate painters, surrounded him, spoiled him, loved him, treated him like a big child with genius. The youngest aspiring poets sought him out. Villaespesa served him as page, and I observed him from a little further off. Rubén Darío himself kept giving us books received from his Modernist friends in America. . . .

The critic Fernández Almagro, biographer of Valle, does not himself hesitate to point out the importance of Darío's presence in Madrid, and shows the relation of the Nicaraguan poet to Valle much as Juan Ramón Jiménez did in the fragment quoted above: [3]

Present at all the conversations of writers who, in flying patrol, formed the *tertulias* of the Café de Madrid or of the Inglés, or of the Horchatería de Candela, was inevitably Rubén Darío. His *Prosas profanas* arrived from Buenos Aires in waves of extraordinary sound. There are some who have known him personally ever since his first journey to Madrid, in 1892, for the ceremonies commemorating the discovery of America. And they will all know him when he returns to Madrid in the early days of 1899 . . . Happy for Valle-Inclán the revelation of this pilgrim friend. They recognize in each other mutual aesthetic tendencies, while in the impassible simplicity of the Spaniard from Nicaragua the impulsive Spaniard of Galicia finds a healthy counterpart.

In his long years of residence in Europe, Darío had made many Spanish friends,[4] and among them perhaps none closer and more brotherly than Valle, who so much admired the American poet. They surely met in 1899, the year in which the Galician writer lost his arm, and it is very possible that they were brought together by another common friend, the unfortunate writer, the picturesque figure of *fin-de-siècle* Bohemia, Alejandro Sawa, then recently returned to Spain from several years' residence in France. Sawa, friend of Verlaine and the symbolist poets, had been, with Gómez Carrillo, the assiduous companion of Darío on his nocturnal adventures in the

Latin Quarter during his first Parisian journey in 1893.[5] Darío, at first disillusioned by the lamentable condition of Spanish literature, speaks years later in his autobiography of the first days spent in the *corte* and calls to mind former companions and new friends, singling out Benavente, Baroja, Maeztu, Ruiz Contreras and, among the young, the Machado brothers, Palomero, Villaespesa, Juan Ramón Jiménez, et cetera.[6] It is perhaps surprising that Valle was not mentioned in his first list, but after evoking Campoamor, Pardo Bazán, Valera and others he had known earlier, he says, a little further on: "We had indescribable culinary sessions, of ambrosia and above all nectar, with the great Ramón María del Valle Inclán, Palomero, Bueno . . ."[7] Nor is it superfluous to mention here, that, walking with Valle in the surroundings of the Casa de Campo of Madrid in the spring of 1899, Darío met for the first time Francisca Sánchez, the humble peasant girl who was to be the distinguished poet's faithful companion for so many years. And once his apartment was established in Marqués de Santa Ana street, Valle came regularly to the house.[8]

In spite of frequent absences of both Darío and Valle from the city, at different times, there must have been many meetings in the Madrid cafés, where literary reunions had their great influence, long since recognized, on the development of Spanish letters of the twentieth century. These took place no doubt in the *Café de Madrid*, in the *Nuevo Café de Levante*, in *El Colonial* and in many others not mentioned here. Both writers, as is well known, were especially devoted to café life: one silent and drinking deep, the other rather more aggressive and exaggerated in speech and gesture. By means of the recollections of other *contertulianos* it is relatively easy to document the encounters of Darío and Valle on the café benches, but we will be satisfied with indicating a few trustworthy testimonials to prove these friendly contacts. From Juan Ramón Jiménez, whose pages of memorabilia about the period must again be emphasized, we have an important piece of prose, never sufficiently praised, not only as a precious document of the time but also for its great beauty of style. We are referring, of course, to "Castillo de quema," that impressive lyric portrait of Valle, published by the poet of Moguer in 1936, the year of his friend's death. Let us look at a few fragments from this substantive and beautiful prose. First, Juan Ramón recreates a characteristic reunion of writers about 1899, at which the principal actors are Darío and Valle:[9]

Valle . . . was reading, declaiming, from a number of *La Ilustración Española y Americana,* the Parnassian alexandrines of *Cosas del Cid* by Rubén Darío. . . . All that matters is alcohol whatever the distillations and labels. Rubén Darío asks again and again for "whiskey and soda" or three star Martel cognac. Everyone here undoubtedly a personality, but J.R.J. concentrates only on Rubén Darío listening ecstatically and on Valle reciting . . . Rubén Darío . . . say only "admirable" and smiles a little with contracted lips. Valle simple, plain, resonant, upright, reads, smiles openly, speaks, smiles, calls out, shouts, smiles, exaggerates, smiles, gets up, smiles, comes and goes, smiles, enters and exits. They go out. The others repeat, "admirable, admirable," in various tones. "Admirable" is the high word of the epoch, "imbecile" the low. With "admirable" and "imbecile" Modernist criticism is constructed. Rubén Darío, for example, admirable; Echegaray, imbecile.

Juan Ramón then refers to the years 1901–1902 when he was in the *Sanatorio del Rosario* and to the writers, Darío and Valle among them, who visited him there, incorporating in this prose important literary considerations about his book *Rimas,* published in 1902, and the aesthetic change it represented. He affirms again the ascendancy of Rubén Darío and Valle, saying: ". . . And Valle influences everyone, like Rubén Darío and with Rubén Darío, who influenced him so greatly, and whom he respects, makes known, celebrates and talks about so contagiously . . ."[10]

And the occasion described by Juan Ramón Jiménez was not by any means the only one when Valle declaimed the master's verses. It has been recorded that at a later date, autumn of 1905, Darío used to attend the *tertulia* at the *Café Colonial,* where he joined old friends, among them the unrepentant dipsomaniac Sawa, and how once again Valle gave a recital, this time directly from the galley proofs of *Cantos de vida y esperanza,* which were just being corrected at the café table, of stanzas of "Canción de otoño en primavera" and "Marcha triunfal."[11] One more bit of evidence will serve to complete the theme of Darío and Valle in the café. It comes from Ricardo Baroja. Although he seems to have made a slight mistake in the date, Baroja has re-created a typical scene in the *Café de Madrid* with the following words:[12]

—And all the people arriving, are they poets?
—All of them. Some of them write on the table covers, others invent novels and stories. In short . . . poets—and the waiter, after a pronouncement,

comes up to the person with the long beard who summoned him by
striking with his cane on the marble table, at the risk of scarring it.

The young man with the Merovingian hair was, as I learned later,
Ramón del Valle-Inclán.

A few young men had entered the café and sat down near the poet at
nearby tables.

. . . .

Another gentleman, a little older, enters and, walking with that springy
roll characteristic of people born in a tropical climate, approaches the
group. He is corpulent, with a large head. His black hair has a slight
tendency to be kinky. Short arms, small hands and feet. He sits down in
the chief place. From my seat opposite the newcomer I observe him. In his
olive skin the little eyes open only slightly, very black, veiled by that
vague nostalgia lent by equatorial sun to men of the Negroid race. His
gestures are slow; he seems to be paralyzed by the waistcoat and jacket
squeezing his torso. He hardly speaks, hardly seems to listen either; but
when Palomero shouts some sarcasm in his cavernous voice, when Benavente makes an epigram and Valle-Inclán a pronouncement, the paralyzed
personage murmurs:

—Admirable! admirable!—and changes his Buddha-like immobility to
ecstasy.

Past the thick lips of his silent mouth flow rivers of beer, and as the table
fills with empty bottles the drinker's eyes grow more opaque.

The indefatigable drinker is the poet Rubén Darío.

If indeed poetic tributes and Valle's correspondence, matters shortly
to be explored, give further proof of the sustained mutual admiration
of the two writers, we do not want to close this section without empha-
sizing other facts which of themselves are useful for measuring the
extent of this literary and friendly relationship. For example, Francisco Contreras, friend and biographer of the American poet, speaks
of his calls on Darío in Madrid somewhere around 1910, and then
states:[13]

. . . One afternoon when I went again to see him, accompanied by Valle-
Inclán, he was more animated. . . . There was a moment of very agreeable
talk, but certainly dominated by the Spanish eloquence of the Marqués de
Bradomín. I remember that, as we were leaving, in the green half light of
early evening, Valle-Inclán said: Rubén is a genius. His observation has
nothing to do with that of common writers, like Blasco Ibáñez, for instance.
He perceives the mysterious interrelation of things. . . .

For reasons to be seen later on, we should like to underline the phrase in which Valle alludes to his friend's extraordinary capacity to perceive *the mysterious interrelation of things*. Other words also of the Galician writer reaffirm and insist upon this exceptional quality in Darío for penetrating the mysterious:[14]

Darío was a child. Immensely good. He lived in a kind of blessed religious dread. He saw things of the other world continuously. Even better, there were no objects not projected thither. I repeat that he was a child. Not proud, nor spiteful, nor ambitious. He had none of the angelic sins. Further removed than anyone from satanic sin, he knew only the sins of the flesh. His soul was pure—completely, utterly pure.

In this connection certain observations of Valle's, made immediately after the Nicaraguan's death and collected by Sassone, are interesting in themselves:[15]

Have you read of it? Poor Rubén!
Don Ramón del Valle-Inclán gave me the sad news, his wizard eyes reddened with weeping.
Horrible! With whom now shall I discuss my *Lámpara maravillosa?* Rubén would have had his whiskey, I my hashish, and we would have plunged deep into mystery. He was a man in contact with the mysterious. And while the master of the *Sonatas* spoke thus, a few tears shone on the crystals of his eyeglasses and his beard trembled beneath his sorrowful voice.

There can be no doubt that the death of Rubén Darío was a profound grief to Valle-Inclán. Melchor Fernández Almagro recalls how he came to know Valle personally on February 7, 1916, and how in his *tertulia* at the *Café del Gato Negro* he paid tribute to the poet so recently vanished: "Valle-Inclán turned the whole conversation into the most fiery encomiums of the person and work of Rubén Darío, expressed . . . in terms of great emotion; and nothing impressed me more in all that Don Ramón said than the deeply sincere grief-stricken tone and the fine declamatory art with which he recited the 'Responso a Verlaine' . . ."[16] In the year of Rubén Darío's death, Valle went to Paris. As a guide he had Pedro Salinas, and we know that he insisted on being taken to see the house where Darío lived in the rue d'Herschelle, thus to pay homage posthumously to the memory of his dear friend.[17]

Poetic tributes

On more than one occasion Rubén Darío revealed his great talent for painting in verse the portrait of a poet. We all remember, for instance, the wonderful verses that succeed in expressing with singular skill the intimate essence of Antonio Machado, a poet more and more admired every day, and we cannot resist the temptation to quote a fragment from the beginning of the poem:

> Misterioso y silencioso
> iba una y otra vez.
> Su mirada era tan profunda
> que apenas se podía ver.

And let us not forget that the Spanish poet in turn wrote two poems to the Nicaraguan.

To Darío we owe also three sincere tributes in verse to Valle-Inclán, which not only treat with authority certain aspects of his work but show as well profound admiration for the man and his writing. Very famous is the "Soneto autumnal al Marqués de Bradomín" (1904) collected in *Cantos de vida y esperanza*, admirable verses which really deserve complete quotation here. In them, from Paris, Rubén accompanies his friend in his development as a writer and affirms aesthetic solidarity with him. This is the poem in which Darío, as he said years later, extols the aristocratic thought of a great talent of the Spanish world.[18]

The second sonnet for Valle-Inclán, the one sometimes called "iconographic" and which appears in *El canto errante* (1907), seems to us less successful, but here are a few significant lines:

> Tengo la sensación de que siento y que vivo
> a su lado una vida más intensa y más dura.
>
> Este gran don Ramón del Valle-Inclán me inquieta,
> y a través del zodíaco de mis versos actuales
> se me esfuma en radiosas visiones de poeta,
>
> O se me rompe en un fracaso de cristales.

In Darío's own opinion,[19] this poem for don Ramón del Valle-Inclán does not succeed in expressing the complexity of the personality, but it does appear in Valle's first book of verse, *Aromas de leyenda* (1907). This latter work is intimately related to *Flor de santidad* which prolongs, on a mystical and legendary base, Christian and pastoral, certain Galician motifs already present in Valle's earlier prose. Because of its musicality and the vague lyric suggestiveness, more symbolist than Parnassian, as well as for its careful formal elaboration, the verse

of *Aromas* evinces an assimilated and very personal Modernism, far
from mere exotic and ornamental externals. Furthermore, Valle uses
metric and stanzaic forms made fashionable by Modernism: verses of
nine syllables, for instance, and tercets on a single rhyme. Here is revealed the age-old soul of Galicia insofar as pertains to poetic mystery.
Valle perceives sensuously, and through all the senses, the native landscape; he shows his sympathy for the humble and destitute people of
Galicia; and in this simple poetry, in minor mode, he gathers vernacu-
lar materials and displays a Franciscan attitude. Gentle poetry, without violence, composed on a nostalgic note, it is regional in the best
sense of the term, while Valle does not ever abandon his position as an
artist. When Darío writes his "Notas sobre Valle-Inclán" he gives us
the following version of his friend's whole work: [20]

Whatever in the poetic work of Valle-Inclán seems most fantastic and
obscure, has a basis of reality. Life stands before the poet, and the poet
transforms it, subtilizes, elevates, multiplies it; in a word, deifies it with all
its inward power and music. He who has no *daimon* cannot do this; and
for this reason I have maintained the superiority of Unamuno to other men
who write purely formal and skillful lyrics.

In the same pages, which reveal great sympathy for Valle and his artistic expression, Darío comments in very favorable terms on the
poetry of *Aromas*, noting their exquisite softness and rhythmic movement.

Later, in 1911, when Rubén was editor of *El Mundial*, and in sad
circumstances of which we shall speak later, the Nicaraguan poet,
again in Paris, sent the often-requested prologue in verse to Valle's
Voces de gesta, the "Balada laudatoria a don Ramón del Valle-Inclán,"
a poem which appears, with its title slightly changed, in modern editions of the aforementioned poetic drama. It is significant that in the
poem the author emphasizes themes and tones characteristic of the
work of his friend, to whom he was united, as he says here, by the
sacred influence of Apollo and the Moon. For the sake of its value as
characterization let us give here the first stanzas:

> Del país de sueño, tinieblas, brillos,
> donde crecen plantas, flores extrañas,
> entre los escombros de los castillos,
> junto a las laderas de las montañas
> donde los pastores en sus cabañas
> rezan, cuando al fuego dormita el can,
> y donde las sombras antiguas van

por cuevas de lobos y de raposas,
ha traído cosas muy misteriosas
DON RAMON MARIA DEL VALLE INCLAN.

Cosas misteriosas, trágicas, raras,
de cuentos obscuros de los antaños,
de amores terribles, crímenes, daños,
como entre vapores de solfataras,
caras sanguinarias, pálidas caras,
gritos ululantes, pena y afán,
infaustos hechizos, aves que van
bajo la amenaza del gerifalte,
dice en versos ricos de oro y esmalte
DON RAMON MARIA DEL VALLE INCLAN.

After Rubén Darío's death, Valle published in 1919 *La pipa de kif*, a revolutionary book and a significant landmark in his literary development. Here it is that he speaks for the first time of the "musa moderna", the new aesthetic of distortion and caricature, which is to predominate in all his later work. With his notorious capacity for renewal, Valle demands for himself new standards: he penetrates the street scene and creates a motley setting of circus and fair populated by strolling players, thieves and other popular types. Left behind are the sumptuous linguistics; the language becomes strident, picturesque and plebeian. The tone is ironic and clever and the poet takes up a position facing the dissonance of the world. It is, besides, a work pointing toward the avant-garde and to the poetic games played in the years after 1920. In spite of such great changes of theme and tone, it is significant that Valle does not forget Rubén Darío, naming him directly in two poems of the book.[21] In the composition "¡Aleluya!", the writer makes fun of the academicians and the purists who are about to be terrified by his acrobatic verses and lyric capers. At this very moment he in turn salutes Rubén Darío, saying:

Darío me alarga en la sombra
Una mano, y a Poe me nombra.

Maga estrella de pentarquía
Sobre su pecho anuncia el día.

Su blanca túnica de Esenio
Tiene las luces del selenio.

¡Sombra de misterioso delta
Vibra en tu honor mi gaita celta!

> ¡Tu amabas las rosas, el vino
> y los amores del camino!
>
> Cantor de Vida y Esperanza,
> Para ti toda mi loanza.
>
> Por el alba de oro, que es tuya,
> ¡Aleluya! ¡Aleluya! ¡Aleluya!

Of course in the transcribed verses are encased various textual quotations from Darío. In parenthesis, we should like to point out that also in *La pipa de kif* Valle incorporates his own "sinfonía en gris mayor",[22] arranged for the modern muse. We refer to the composition entitled "Marina norteña," which includes the following illustrative verses:

> Escruta el mar con la mirada quieta
> Un marinero desde el muelle. Brilla
> Con el traje de aguas su silueta
> Entre la boina gris, toda amarilla.
>
> Viento y lluvia de mar. La luna flota
> Tras el nublado. Apenas se presiente,
> Lejana, la goleta que derrota
> Cortando el arco de la luz poniente.
>
> Se ilumina el cuartel. Vagas siluetas
> Cruzan tras las ventanas enrejadas,
> Y en el gris de la tarde las cornetas
> Dan su voz como rojas llamaradas.
>
> . . . .
>
> Las olas rompen con crestón de espuma
> Bajo el muelle. Los barcos cabecean
> Y agigantados en el caos de bruma
> Sus jarcias y sus cruces fantasean.
>
> La triste sinfonía de las cosas
> Tiene en la tarde un grito futurista:
> De una nueva emoción y nuevas glosas
> Estéticas, se anuncia la conquista.

Letters of Valle-Inclán to Rubén Darío

In this section we shall concern ourselves rather summarily with what has so far been published of Valle's correspondence with Darío, letters confirming once more the cordiality that always characterized the personal relationship of the two writers. As we shall see, one of these communications goes beyond the mere theme of friendship, since in it is given some precious information concerning the real genesis of Valle's *Luces de bohemia*. In 1943 Alberto Ghiraldo published four letters written by Valle to Darío,[23] and more recently Dictino Alvarez Hernández, who had at his disposal the documents belonging to the Seminario-Archivo Rubén Darío in Madrid, has enriched this correspondence by bringing to light seven other Valle letters and four of his wife's, Josefina Blanco, all of them addressed to the Nicaraguan poet.[24] At the same time it is well to note here that the archives mentioned, very rich in letters *to* Darío, are on the other hand relatively poor as regards letters from the poet himself.

Most of the letters making up this short correspondence are concerned with editorial matters. The first, undated, reproduced by Ghiraldo, treats of an introduction in behalf of M. Chaumier, translator of *Romance de lobos* and Consul General of France in Spain. Apparently, at an earlier date, Valle had written to Darío asking him to influence Rémy de Gourmont so as to assure publication of the work in *Le Mercure de France*. And actually, a few years later, in 1914, under the title of *La geste des loups: Comédie barbare en trois journées*, it appeared in the French review. It is worth mentioning that, in introducing M. Chaumier, Valle wrote: ". . . in whom you will find a true connoisseur of our literature, who knows how to look even into the esoteric depth of your verses that seem so arcane to many of our academics, critics and poets."[25] Two communications of 1907[26] reveal to what extent Valle tried to intervene in the publication of *El canto errante*. From a letter of the publisher, Gregorio Pueyo, dated August 10, 1907, and collected by Ghiraldo,[27] we learn that Darío himself had written Valle about this matter. In his efforts Valle took great pains to place the original of the book with Pueyo, and even thought of taking charge himself of the proposed edition. It turned out, nevertheless, that Darío's new work was published ultimately by the firm of Pérez Villavivencio, which Valle, on a postcard dated later, described as "a collection of thieves", who had cheated him of a thousand pesetas.[28]

In 1911 began the publication of the *Mundial Magazine*, an undertaking destined to bring painful problems to Darío in his position as director of such a sumptuous review. Two letters copied by Ghiraldo[29] and various others published by Alvarez[30] treat precisely of the insertion of *Voces de gesta* in *Mundial* and the payment thereof, the price being left by the author for Darío to determine. The three acts of the work were, in effect, printed in that review, published in Paris. In the correspondence Valle asks Darío urgently, over and over again, for the promised prologue in verse for his books. For a time the printing of the *de luxe* edition intended by Valle was held up because the invocation to go in the first pages did not come. Although it has not been possible to authenticate the fact, we suspect that the first edition of *Voces de gesta* (1911) appeared without Darío's verses, but in the second, published the next year, the "Balada laudatoria que envía al autor el alto poeta Rubén" was included.

Of greater literary interest and truly sensational for reasons to be shown later, is a letter written by Valle to Darío in 1909. The first to reproduce it was Oliver Belmás[31] and it was later published in the book, already quoted, of Dictino Alvarez.[32] The most eloquent passage is the following:

Dear Darío:

I come to you after having been at the house of our poor Alejandro Sawa. I wept over the dead man, for him, for myself and for all poor poets. I can do nothing; nor can you; but if a few of us join together we could do something.

Alejandro leaves an unfinished book. The best he ever wrote. A journal of hopes and tribulations.

The frustration of his desire to publish it and a letter cancelling a contract of sixty pesetas for contributions to *El Liberal* drove him mad these last days. Madness of despair. He wanted to kill himself. His was the end of a king of tragedy: mad, blind and raging.

Now, neither Oliver nor Alvarez seems to have remarked on the literary importance of these honest lines, motivated by the sad circumstances of Sawa's death, a friend, as already indicated, of both writers. Here, then, is the true genesis, in 1909, of *Luces de bohemia*, an *esperpentic* work published years later, in 1920, created out of authentic reality and inspired by a concrete painful event that in fact moved Valle quite deeply.[33]

Let us see, very briefly, how certain details of such a lamentable event and the reaction Valle felt at Sawa's tragic end, passed with time into his creative work. As is well known, the character of Max Estrella, protagonist of *Luces de bohemia*, is none other than Sawa, who wrote several naturalistic novels and a volume of short pieces, published posthumously with the significant title: *Iluminaciones en la sombra* (1910). This is a miscellaneous collection of pieces, compositions of different dates, which serve to complete the intimate portrait of the

of death with the Marqués de Bradomín, already an old man. The portrait of Darío also is authentic: his silences and the laconic statements of "admirable," even to his "idol mask" and the "vast and sinister sadness sculptured in the likeness of Aztec idols." Significant, too, in its literary and personal context, is the noble letter already quoted that Valle wrote Darío in 1909 about the pathetic death of Alejandro Sawa, whose figure, though partly legendary and on the outskirts of the literary revival, brought to a head by writers of greater talent, is still not devoid of interest.[37]

Traces of Darío in the work of Valle-Inclán

Looking back over the long road travelled up to now at the many evidences, some merely anecdotal and others more literary, that are useful in indicating the extent of literary and friendly relations between Darío and Valle-Inclán, there is definite interest in pointing out how different, concrete recollections of the Nicaraguan's work served Valle in the enrichment of his own writing. Verbal traces are innumerable and even thematic ones offer abundant harvest.[38] In showing some of these reminiscences, we are not unaware of the possibility of mutual influence, but for the moment let us limit ourselves to examining a few passages that seem derived from the influence Darío had on the Spanish writer.[39] We are definitely not proposing here a traditional study of literary sources, but for the moment merely wish to isolate a method of composition in Valle and the legitimate means by which an author inspires an initiated reader offering him an opportunity to be an accomplice of the creator himself. As is well known, Valle used to embroider his work with intentional and voluntary textual memories of other writers. Sometimes he did this to achieve a more biting satire, as in *Los cuernos de don Friolera*, *Las galas del difunto* and *Tirano Banderas*. At other times he did it for atmosphere and to offer authentic documentation for unfamiliar epochs. Of such is, of course, the already familiar case of accusation of plagiarism brought by Casares,[40] who found in the *Sonata de primavera* fragments taken directly from the memoirs of Casanova, a source admitted by Valle himself in the text of the work.[41] On the other hand, it is legitimate to believe, as stated by Emma Susana Speratti Piñero, who has so subtly studied particular sources and Valle's use of them, that he delighted also in mocking the learned and putting off the scent those near-sighted critics who jealously dedicated themselves to discovering immediate sources.[42] That

is to say that on more than one occasion Valle intentionally made
literature out of literature, often confessing by artful indications the
paternity of the alien texts used in the great mosaic of his work.

As has been already said, certain works of Valle's first period, above
all the *Sonatas*, show without obscuring the individuality of the author,
a clear and decided Modernist influence. This juxtaposition persists,
although with an important change of attitude, in later works like
Cuento de abril. La cabeza del dragón, La marquesa Rosalinda and
many others. In Valle's stories antedating the *Sonatas*, with their com-
plicated elaboration, as is confirmed by Speratti Piñero in the case of
the *Sonata de otoño*,[43] the one nearest to the same sensual and volup-
tuous style is "Augusta," collected later in *Corte de amor*.

No one can forget the refined and courtly ambience in which the
characters of the *Sonatas* languidly move. To delightful frivolity and
great elegance are added typical examples of *fin-de-siècle* decadence,
as well as the constant search for rare and exquisite sensations. Valle
cultivates the characteristic mixture of the profane and the sacred, a
motif so dear to the Modernists, the two extremes being present in
compositions like "El reino interior" and "Ite missa est" by Darío. And
lastly, reality is embellished by many aesthetical procedures. As we
all know, around this literature inspired more by art than life, gather
many decorative materials of Modernism—swans and peacocks—and
it would not be superfluous to mention here that concerning this precious style, essentially poetic and musical, Darío once wrote: "Valle-
Inclán is called decadent because he writes a worked and polished prose
of the finest formal excellence . . ."[44] All the same, the *Sonatas* are
small masterpieces written in a manner now somewhat out of fashion,
of which years later Valle himself made fun, and in which the author
perhaps paid excessive tribute to the formalist literature of the age. It
is not surprising, then, that much is owed to the ascendancy of Darío
and to the many French authors they both knew. Many images seem
to have a more or less direct reminiscence of Darío. For example, Valle
writes in the *Sonata de invierno*: "With the warm chorus of the trum-
pets rose shrill neighing, and in the street resounded, valiant and
martial, the clang of horses' hooves, that noble sound of arms and
paladins belonging to the old romances." It is immediately clear how
this synaesthetic image, several times elaborated in the same work and
in later ones,[45] is related to certain verses of Darío's poem "Marcha
triunfal".[46] Other fragments bear no less an echo of Darío and of the

Modernist motifs put in circulation by the American poet. Let us look at a few of the many that might be cited:[47]

(1) ... From the drawing room could be glimpsed the garden, motionless beneath the moon, which veiled in a pale clarity the languid tops of the cypresses and the balconies of the terrace, where in other days the peacock opened its chimeric and storied fan. (*Sonata de primavera*)

(2) The soft and gentle air, an air to conjure sighs, passed murmuring, and far away among the motionless myrtles, stirred the wavelets of a pool ... (*Sonata de primavera*)

(3) ... The salon was gilded in the French style, feminine and luxurious. Garlanded cupids, nymphs in lace, gallant hunters and stags with branching antlers peopled the tapestry on the wall, and on the consoles graceful groups in porcelain, pastoral dukes enlacing the flower-decked waists of peasant marquesses ... (*Sonata de primavera*)

(4) ... That night she howled in my arms like a faun of olden days ... (*Sonata de invierno*)

Furthermore, in the *Sonata de estío*, where there are clear allusions to Bécquer and Silva, Valle writes: "... with that smile which a poet of today would have called a winged strophe of snow and roses." Is this a definite reminiscence of Darío?

In 1904 Valle publishes *Flor de santidad*. He is quite conscious of having done something different and explains it in a letter to his friend Torcuato Ulloa.[48] The aristocratic world of the *Sonatas* has disappeared, and another has been substituted for it: primitive, elemental, age-old, popular. The background is Galician, a landscape nearly always sombre; the motifs are consistently superstitious and supernatural; the regionalism artistic and evocative, not descriptive; the structural axis of the short novel is the contrast established between the pious soul of Adega and the more sensual and vengeful one of the pilgrim. Although in *Flor de santidad* the merely literary and Parnassian element recedes, there is no doubt that Darío's prose is still influencing Valle's, as Raimundo Lida saw clearly.[49] In this work, more poem than novel, the same ideal of stylistic perfection persists, now at the service of a Galician theme, and an essential Modernism in process of transformation is revealed especially in the sustained lyrical beautifying of the landscape and the figure of Adega. In this accomplished work occurs one short passage which interests us here because it seems to carry an echo of Darío's "Sinfonía en gris mayor":

They went on in silence. The path was full of cloudy pools, reflecting the moon, and the frogs, chanting in that silver light their monotonous senile song at the brink, leapt into the water as soon as footsteps came near. . . .

The style in the three novels of the Carlist wars (1908–1909) wherein the main interest consists in their being a first step leading, years later, to the great novels of the *Ruedo Ibérico*,[50] does not in general continue the Modernism of earlier and later works. The exigencies of the subject are simply different. We should like, however, to call attention now to an interesting reminiscence of Darío which appears first in *El resplandor de la hoguera* and again in *Gerifaltes de antaño*, the last volume of the trilogy with a title taken directly from a verse of Darío.[51] In the first novel mentioned, the Field Marshall, Don Enrique España, moves with his staff to the palace of Redín, the property of an aged countess of the same name. In a few pages, slightly more Modernist in tone, Valle introduces us to the interior of the palace and to Eulalia, the granddaughter, companion to her venerable grandmother. This name does not appear here for the first time in Valle's work, but the following words are interesting:

Eulalia, if at any moment she was unobserved, would look at herself in the mirror, put a flower on her breast and, on her grandmother's clavichord play the waltz to which in other days she had so often danced when her parents gave parties at their palace in Madrid. . . .

And then a little further on:

O gay music scattered by that ancient clavichord full of sorrows! Eulalia had forgotten it, and suddenly thought she could hear it very far away, with the vagueness of a dream, under the glance of a hussar bearing on his dolman the cross of Santiago . . . without finishing the waltz she leans her forehead on the ivories of the clavichord which gives out a deep groan:
    —How mad! how mad! . . . and he married!

The traces of Darío are obvious: the poem "El Clavicordio de la abuela," a composition not included in *Prosas profanas*, where because of date and tone it might belong, but collected in *Poema del otoño y otros poemas* (1910) the heroine of which, the marquesita Rosalinda, gave Valle at a later time the title of his eighteenth-century farce. And, so the crossing of reminiscences may not elude us, in the last work of the series the Duke of Ordax calls the granddaughter "divine Eulalia," an epithet carrying us back again to "Era un aire suave."[52]

Between 1909 and 1914 Valle-Inclán published a series of books independent yet related, being works for the theatre in verse. If *Voces de gesta* (1912) is somewhat solemn in purpose, with tragic and epic overtones, the other pieces (*Cuento de abril*, 1909, and *La marquesa Rosalinda*, 1912) of that intermediate period show, in various degrees and intent, a certain Modernist residue, especially as regards their decorative background. In the delightful *Cuento de abril*, for instance, there is manifest a whole refined and courtly atmosphere: Provençal gardens propitious for love, fountains around which peacocks spread their tails, the chorus of *azafatas* (ladies-in-waiting) that play in this exotic and artificial world. Although the principal dramatic motive, surely very weak, is the opposition quickly established between the ascetic customs of Castile and the sensuality of the Court of Love presided over by the Princess Imberal, of greater interest is the fine and elegant atmosphere of affected discretion and gallantry, where the relation to aspects of *Prosas profanas* is clear. The following stanzas of "Preludio," for example, anticipate the tonality of this light and graceful theatrical work: [53]

> La divina puerta dorada
> del jardín azul de ensueño
> os abre mi vara encantada
> por deciros un cuento abrileño.
>
> . . . .
>
> Bajo un vuelo de abejas de oro,
> las gentiles rosas de Francia,
> al jardín azul y sonoro,
> dan el tesoro de su fragancia.
>
> Fragancia de labios en flor,
> que al reír modulan un trino,
> labios que besa el ruiseñor
> con la luz de su trino divino.
>
> ¡Oh, la fragancia de la risa
> fragante escala musical,
> que al alma leve la brisa,
> le brinda su verso de coral!
>
> ¡Oh, rosa de la risa loca,
> que rima el teclado de su son

con la púrpura de la boca
y las fugas del Ave-Ilusión!

At this transitional stage there emerge two of Valle's works that must be judged supremely important, although in fact they have been very little studied: *La marquesa Rosalinda* and *La cabeza del dragón*, the latter written in prose in 1909 although not collected in book form until 1914 with a slight change of title.[54] The interesting thing, for purposes of this article, is to point out that in both farces persists the Modernist décor which Valle-Inclán is soon to abandon forever. The thing that differentiates these works from earlier ones is the author's new posture. A definitely humorous and scoffing attitude tinges the Modernism of *La marquesa Rosalinda*. The viewpoint, grotesque and jovial at the same time, will change in time to sarcasm and grimace of the later years. Even earlier, in *La cabeza del dragón*, a *farsa infantil* as the author later baptised it, there are perceptible indications of new stylistic modes, in bits turned frankly towards caricature, although there is still lacking the moralistic dimension that will appear later. Nor is this farce out of tune, delicious satire as it is on fairy tales and novels of chivalry, in the volume *Tablado de marionetas*, the subtitle of which, "for the education of princes," is also meaningful. And if in *La cabeza del dragón* some aspects of the style of the *esperpentos* are anticipated and the Vallesque sense of humour is shown in high relief somewhere between comic and grotesque, yet the Versailles décor still appears. A great part of the action takes place in the fantastic kingdom of King Micomicón, and certain stage directions recall closely, even verbally, Rubén Darío:

. . . Rose garden and marble stairway, where peacocks spread their tails. A lake and two harmonious swans. . . .

In the royal gardens. The peacock, with tail always spread like a fabulous rainbow fan, stands on the marble stairway trimmed with roses. At its foot, the silver gondola with ivory canopy. And the fair swans sailing at the prow, like music in their lyric curve. . . .

Of capital importance in all this intermediate stage is, as said before, *La marquesa Rosalinda*, presented in 1912 and first published in book form a year after. The verse of this charming farce is clearly Modernist, both in form and in decorative background. The Darío contagion is decisive, in the sense that no aspect of the refined Versailles ambience is lacking, and all the characters, typical of balls and gallantry, move with steps of a minuet. The note of idle frivolity and courtly discretion is presented with mastery. It is easy to appreciate how Valle has incorporated in his "sentimental and grotesque" farce all the familiar fauna and flora of Modernism, but the most important thing is that at the same time he departs from this frequented path with tonality openly burlesque. The nine-syllable verses of the prelude, dated 1911 when they were published in Darío's *Mundial*, show an intentional departure from Modernist solemnity. Of course, echoes of de Banville are not hard to find in Darío and other Modernists, particularly in Lugones, but let us see how, with tinkling rhymes, Valle tells us his little story:

> Y sollocen otros poetas
> sobre los cuernos de la lira,
> con el ritmo de las piruetas
>
> . . . .
>
> Por el sendero la vestía
> la noche, de niebla y armiños
> y la luciérnaga seguía
> en su falda, haciéndome guiños.
>
> . . . .
>
> Enlazaré las rosas frescas
> con que se viste el vaudeville
> y las rimas funambulescas
> a la manera de Banville.
>
> . . . .
>
> Versalles pone sus empaques,
> Aranjuez, sus albas rientes,
> y un grotesco de miriñaques
> don Francisco Goya y Lucientes.

This lightness being noted, *La marquesa Rosalinda* is also a seedbed of suggestions which Valle will take possession of later: the theme of honor in the theater of Calderón, as well as the conventional personages of the *commedia dell'arte* and their masks, which had been revived also in Modernism. Even in the moon motif rises an echo of Laforgue's irony and of Lugones, the much admired author of *Lunario sentimental*. Verses spoken by Arlequín in *La Marquesa Rosalinda* are pertinent to this:

> ¡Oh, luna de poetas y de orates,
> por tu estela argentina

mi alma peregrina
con un ansia ideal de disparates!

. . . .

¿Quién el poder a descubrir acierta
de tu cara de plata,
de tus ojos de muerta
y tu nariz chata?

. . . .

¡Hilandera divina de sonetos!
El barro de mi alma se aureola
con tu luz enigmática,
y te saluda con la cabriola
de una bruja sabática:
Luna que de soñar guardas las huellas,
cabalística luna de marfil,
tú escribes en lo azul moviendo estrellas:
¡Nihil!

It would be truly unproductive to collect the infinite number of echoes, even verbal ones, of Darío in this work, but it should at least be mentioned that Doña Estrella, Rosalinda's beautiful daughter, was locked up in a convent lest she overshadow her mother. On one occasion the *butterfly* escapes, although soon forced to return to her *cage* to sigh over her troubles and die with her *head under her wing*. She even exclaims, "Oh, to be a bird in the sky/ to fly, fly, fly!" And the charm is that Valle, point counterpoint, mingles with Doña Estrella's lyric raptures the ironic commentaries of the Dueña and the Marquis. Nor is the lovelorn page omitted. As in *Cuento de abril* the motif is repeated of a young girl waiting, and the opposition between Versailles and Spain appears again because in Spain the Marquis is given the evil eye, he who earlier smiled at the blunders of husbands in the Spanish theater. This change into a heroic Castilian Rosalinda attributes to the *autos de fe* and the plays of Calderón.

Also with eighteenth-century surrounding in which Italian notes are combined with the more classic Spanish, cultured as well as popular, is the successful and complex *Farsa italiana de la enamorada del rey* (1920). This is a work constructed predominantly out of literature, especially that of Cervantes, in which standards of poetry and fantasy finally triumph. The literary satire is truly witty; various planes of reality and illusion cross one another; again Versailles is contrasted with Spanish usage ("This Spanish race loves only realities;/For the native Iberian, and more and more hirsute,/to name the Absolute is to name his mother"). Guillermo Díaz-Plaja has intelligently noted[55] how the imprint of Darío persists in this farce, particularly as regards the parody of "Sonatina" in the verses of Maese Lotario, which recount the loves of Mari-Justina, whose dreams "are clothed/in the sad blue of the ideal." Because of its French novelties and its *"pies excomulgados,"* the alexandrines of the puppet-master did not, of course, escape censure from the learned and rhetorical Don Furibundo, who for his part pretends to an academic chair.

In the new direction taken by his work from here on, Valle naturally abandons the sumptuous and exotic motifs derived from Darío and the Modernist school. Let us remember, however, that in *La pipa de kif* he respectfully salutes the American poet who in key scenes of *Luces de bohemia* even figures in person. It is worth noting moreover how Valle, in his great *esperpentic* novel *Tirano Banderas* (1926) sounds intentional echoes of Darío's poetry. The illustrious Spaniard Don Celes, baroque and pompous, flatters the tyrant and calls him by way of encomium: "Professor of energy, as they say in our Diario!" The pointed ironic intention stands out in relief if we recall Darío's poem, "A Roosevelt," which appears in *Cantos de vida y esperanza.* Again, to characterize the fatuity of this same Don Celes, Valle has very closely in mind some verses of "Pórtico" when he writes:

The Spaniard experienced breath-taking conceit, an overwhelming sensation of pride and reverence. The bluster of famous sonorous names clattered like hames upon his chest....

and in another later visit to the grotesque Minister of Spain: ". . . he spread himself like a peacock with marvelous tail." In the tremendous passages where Valle satirizes the diplomatic corps, direct quotations from Darío can be found. First, Aníbal Roncalí, Minister of Ecuador, recommends a meeting under the presidency of the Minister of Spain, saying: "The young eagles which spread their wings for heroic flight, grouped around the maternal eagle;" then to top it all, the Spanish diplomat, who has developed an anything but healthy passion for the representative of the Ecuadorian government, calling forth the following observation from another colleague: "Lyrical, sentimental, sensitive, emotional, exclaims the Swan of Nicaragua! Because of this you will not be able to separate diplomatic action from the Spanish

Minister's flirtation." Thus it is that even in his eagerness to mock the tragic reality of America, Valle again adapts the verses of Rubén Darío, now in an ironic context.[56]

Some final observations

In the preceding pages we have seen only a few reminiscences, thematic and verbal, of Darío in various works of Valle-Inclán. The Spanish writer's profound admiration for the Nicaraguan poet actually goes much deeper and widens to embrace many attitudes towards the world and literature in general. That is to say, it is by no means limited to the use of the so-called decorative motifs of the Modernist school, those same aesthetic symbols that lose force in the hands of followers without true poetic talent. On the contrary, the harmonious swans and divine princesses are concentrated symbolic forms chosen in protest against the flat and shabby reality which both writers knew all too well. In the spiritual complexity implied in what we call Modernism, a movement of profound ideological content, there is always a desire to go above exterior circumstance, creating and affirming a world of eternal artistic beauty, uncontaminated by the bourgeois materialism of the times. Rubén and Valle, by rejecting in their work earlier well-trodden paths, reacted positively against a reality dominated by mediocrity, and defending themselves with these aesthetic weapons, fought the vulgarity of the moment. Thus it is that both are fundamentally rebellious and each in his way opposes the conventionalities of the epoch, declaring his personal disenchantment with the vulgar, common world surrounding him.[57] Once again it is the acute sensibility of Juan Ramón Jiménez that manages to visualize even in *Prosas profanas* a dimension often underrated in Darío. In his lyric portrait the Spanish poet says:[58]

Today, when [Darío] is back with his golden spear of harmony, with the same roses on his breast, everyone sings his triumphal march. Taking off the armour, we have seen the heart. I had already seen it when, drunk with melancholy, he sang his *Prosas profanas*. Few have said it, but Rubén is a man who feels; his verses have a celestial and sad depth, even among the reddest silks and bodies fragrant with sun.

In its most lasting aspects, as a fruitful lesson in aesthetics and a linguistic revitalization, Modernism was not merely a squandering of empty symbols, but a noble, passionate and selfless gesture to spread supreme artistic beauty and aristocracy of thought. It is true that Valle begins in the *Sonatas*, for instance, by stylizing the lovelier side of things, only later to rid himself of his complex of princesses—a phrase of Salinas[59]—and create a different beauty, more involved, if you like, and differently directed. It is worthwhile asking, however, if the method is not in essence the same, although around 1920 the weapons of protest used before no longer sufficed for Valle. What can be stated with confidence is that a poetic quality always characterized Valle's work, no matter whether beautiful princesses or deformed puppets peopled it, for in both instances he maintains a clear lyric tension. Ultimately, then, the thing that Valle-Inclán found in his friend Darío was a deep affinity in the conception of art as an absolute value, and a system of thought oriented towards the mysterious very like that which the Galician writer expounded in *La lámpara maravillosa*.

Like any conscientious poet, Rubén Darío had an aesthetic of words, that is, *del verbo*. It may perhaps not be idle to transcribe here a well-known passage from the "Palabras liminares" of *Prosas profanas*:

Since each word has a soul, in each verse besides the verbal harmony there is an ideal melody. Often the music is that of the idea alone.

The screaming of the three hundred geese, Silvano, will not keep you from playing your enchanting flute, provided that your friend, the nightingale is pleased with your melody. When she is not by to listen, close your eyes and play for those who dwell in your inner kingdom.

Resuming these same ideas in "Dilucidaciones," prologue to *El Canto errante*, Darío says: ". . . I have wanted to go towards the future, always under the divine rule of music—music of ideas, music of the word (*del verbo*)." In this context we may remember how Rubén Darío, with his sure criteria, saw the poet in Unamuno ("to be a poet is to look through the doors of mystery and come back with a glimmer of the unknown in the eyes"), and in these same prophetic pages the American poet said: "In Unamuno we see the necessity which requires the soul of the true poet to express itself rhythmically, to tell his thoughts and feelings in a musical mode." Having rejected the "legion of piano players" and with a mind open to all forms of beauty, Darío in his evaluation of Unamuno as a poet insists again on musicality as essential:[60]

The thing that stands out in this case is: the necessity of song. After wearying the arms and blunting axes in the flowering fields of lucubration, comes a moment when it is necessary to seek a peaceful corner of freshness

and green to rest in, where the limpid soul may listen to the nightingales'
song. These nightingales, like the bird of paradise the monk of the legend
heard sing, know of the eternal, of that which has nothing to do with the
changing and ephemeral in our earthly life or our rapid passage through
existence, which is that of a rainbow bubble.

The necessity of song: song is the single thing which frees us from what
Maeterlinck calls the tragic of every day. Insofar as time passes and in
spite of the triumphs of material advances, Orphic omnipotence grows and
becomes always more invincible. And the poet sees passing in triumph,
beside the aviator, the conquering flight of the ode.

Toward the end of his life Darío wrote his little-known autobiographical novel, *El oro de Mallorca*, in which the protagonist-mirror is a
famous musician. Baring his tormented spirit in this human document,
Benjamín Itaspes says to himself in one of his many introspective
moments:

Art, like his religious tendency, was another preserver of life. When he
submerged or let his soul float in it, he felt the emancipation of another
and higher world. Music was like an ocean in the waters of which, subtle
and spiritual essence as they were, he acquired the strength of immortality
and something like vibrations of eternal electricity. All the visible universe
and much of the invisible was shown in rhythmic sonority, like a perceptible angelic language, the absolute meaning of which we cannot embrace because of the weight of our material mechanism. The vast forest,
like the system of heavenly mechanics, possessed a melodic and harmonious
language that only demiurgic beings could perceive: Pythagoras and
Wagner were right. Music in its immense concept embraced all, material
and spiritual, and for this reason the Greeks also understood in these terms
sublime Poetry, *La Creadora*. . . .

The mention of Pythagoras and Wagner is not casual, and makes explicit the longing to be submerged in the cosmic harmony through a
series of magic correspondences and poetic associations. Another text,
in this case much earlier, found in the story "El velo de la reina Mab"
(*Azul* . . . .) confirms this same desire for absolute experience and
immersion in the great whole. Again it involves a musician:

. . . I listen to all harmonies, from the lyric of Terpander to the orchestral
fantasies of Wagner. My ideals shine in the midst of my audacities, those
of a man inspired. I have perception like the philosopher who heard the
music of the stars. All sounds can be imprisoned, all echoes are susceptible
to combination. Everything lies within the boundaries of my chromatic
scales.

The vibrating light is a hymn and the melody of the forest has an echo in my heart. From the roar of the tempest to the song of a bird, all is mingled and woven into infinite cadence.

And does not Valle surrender, from the beginning, to this mysterious power of the word, with all its musical and ultralogical radiations? Does he not long to pull the curtain back and approach the enigma of a world visible and invisible through a similar system of thought? In the Spanish writer this same passion for the musical and emotive word does indeed exist. These lines date from 1902: "According to Gautier, words acquire by their sound a value that dictionaries cannot determine. In sound some words are like diamonds, others gleam like phosphorus, others float like mist. . . ."[61] And in this connection will inevitably be remembered the short chapter of *La lámpara maravillosa* entitled, "El milagro musical." From the same book of aesthetics, a book full of verbal resonance from Darío and above all from the introduction in verse to *Cantos de vida y esperanza*, we quote two fragments where the clear meaning excuses us from further comment:

(1) The enchantment rests precisely on the mystery by which it is produced. Wherever the words cannot reach with their meanings, flow the waves of their music. . . . To the delight of their ideological essence is added the delight of their musical essence, numen of a higher category. . . .

(2) Let us seek out the mysterious and subtle allusion that shakes us like a breeze and lets us glimpse a secret meaning beyond human thought. . . . Let us make of all our life a sort of strophe, where the interior rhythm awakes indefinable sensations, wiping out the ideological significance of the words.

Moreover, in *La lámpara maravillosa*, the orthodox, neo-Platonic and above all Gnostic elements have been fully recognized. In this book Valle confesses to having given way to the temptation of practicing the occult sciences. It is worthwhile to remind ourselves again that Darío also was an initiate in the esoteric worlds of Spiritualism and the Cabala. At the news of the death of the American poet, as we have already mentioned, Valle lamented that he now had no one with whom to discuss his new book on aesthetics. In *Luces de bohemia*, furthermore, we find the conversation already alluded to, between Don Latino and Rubén Darío about their common theosophical studies and celestial mathematics. That is to say, both writers are related also, in a complex series of correspondences, by a current of thought that would permit them to penetrate the most arcane mysteries of the universe and achieve, by seeking the occult meaning in the whole of creation, a desired communion with the harmony of the Great Whole. Faced with the indecipherable, both were aroused and both tried, sometimes by the same road, to approach the secret and find the key to this mysterious harmony. Let us listen to the Valle of *La lámpara maravillosa:*

Knowledge of a grain of wheat, with all it evokes, would give us full knowledge of the universe. . . . Into this world of evocation only poets penetrate, because in their eyes everything has a religious significance, near to its unique significance. There where other men find only differences, poets discover the luminous interweaving of a secret harmony. The poet reduces the number of allusions without transcendence to a divine allusion loaded with meanings. A bee loaded with honey!

And a little further on he reaffirms: ". . . The thorn of the bramble and the venom of the serpent tell me a secret of harmony as surely as maiden, rose and star." For the rest, in the immense gallery of Vallesque personages, some professed theosophy and it is worth recalling here at least one of them, belonging to his last period. The antithesis to the dark dictator Santos Banderas is the illuminate, Don Roque de Cepeda, angelic figure and apostle of the redeeming light. Let us not forget that for the invention of this character, Valle was inspired to some extent by the figure of Francisco I. Madero, to whom theosophical or spiritualist ideas have been attributed. The author tells us of the man's profound religion, "forged of mystic and Hindu intuitions", and, resuming certain key ideas of *La lámpara maravillosa*, he then says: "An adept in theosophical doctrines, he sought in the furthest depths of his consciousness a relationship with the consciousness of the universe . . ." Thus, both Rubén Darío and Valle-Inclán, anxious to penetrate the occult meaning of things, turned towards the mysteries and sought exactly this unity between their own consciousness and that of the universe.[62]

In the preceding pages we believe to have offered ample proof, both in the form of concrete evidence and in quotations, of the mutual admiration that existed between Darío and Valle and the many ways in which each corresponded to the other. The two famous writers, united in a lasting friendship and in the supreme adventure of art, have achieved their portion of artistic immortality. Finally, an opportune epilogue to this modest tribute may be given in these verses of Rubén

Darío, where the inner meaning can be related equally well to the personality of the Spaniard:

¡Yo soy el amante de ensueños y formas
que viene de lejos y va al porvenir!
(*El canto errante*, "La canción de los pinos").

NOTES

[1] Angel Lázaro, *Semblanzas y ensayos* (Puerto Rico, 1963), p. 94.

[2] Juan Ramón Jiménez, *El trabajo gustoso* (México, 1961), pp. 227–228.

[3] Melchor Fernández Almagro, *Vida y literatura de Valle Inclán* (Madrid, 1943), pp.50–51.

[4] Concerning the theme of Rubén Darío and his Spanish friendships, the pages of Antonio Oliver Belmás are especially useful (*Este otro Rubén Darío* [Barcelona, 1960], pp. 141–194) and those of Dictino Alvarez Hernández (*Cartas de Rubén Darío* [Madrid, 1963], pp. 47–106.)

[5] Rubén Darío, "Autobiografía", *Obras Completas* (Madrid, 1950), I, pp. 102–104.

[6] *Ibid.*, pp. 141–142.

[7] *Ibid.*, p. 144.

[8] For more complete details about this significant encounter, see Carmen Conde, *Acompañando a Francisca Sánchez* (Managua, 1964), pp. 10–12.

[9] Juan Ramón Jiménez, "Ramón del Valle-Inclán (Castillo de quema)," *Pájinas escojidas. Prosa* (Madrid, 1958), pp. 133–134.

[10] *Ibid.*, p. 136.

These pages of Juan Ramón Jiménez are rich in literary and aesthetic intimacies, which have changed, with time, into literary history. In relation to the theme with which we are now concerned, we would not fail to mention the affection Valle felt for the work of Espronceda (no matter how pitilessly he satirizes him in *Tirano Banderas*), who, Valle proclaimed, saved him from d'Annunzio. Juan Ramón adds further that Galicia saved Valle from exotic Modernism. And lastly, how can one fail to remember the fine appreciation of Valle's style and language given by the poet of Moguer!

[11] Juan Antonio Cabezas, *Rubén Darío. Un poeta y una vida* (Madrid, 1944) pp. 235–236.

[12] Ricardo Baroja, *Gente de 98* (Madrid, 1952), p. 17 and p. 19.

[13] Francisco Contreras, *Rubén Darío. Su vida y su obra* (Santiago de Chile, 1937), p. 129.

[14] Francisco Madrid, *La vida altiva de Valle Inclán* (Buenos Aires, 1943), p. 292. For his part, Pedro Henríquez Ureña ("Don Ramón del Valle-Inclán", *Obra crítica* [México, 1960], p. 685) recalls the following words of Valle referring to Darío: "He was essentially good," said Don Ramón. "He had human failings. But no angelic sins: not anger, nor pride, nor envy."

[15] Felipe Sassone, "El lírico de la raza latina", *La ofrenda de España a Rubén*

Darío (Editorial América, 1916), p. 61. Juan José Llovet records the same reference, "Ha muerto el pontífice . . .", *Ibid.*, p. 114.

[16] Melchor Fernández Almagro, "Valle-Inclán, de cerca", *Indice*, IX (núms. 74–75, abril y mayo de 1954), p. 1 and p. 19.

[17] Fernández Almagro, *Vida y literatura de Valle Inclán*, p. 188. This same friend of Valle's has also said: ". . . Valle-Inclán feels wounded to the depths of his heart. No other writer of his time has he loved and admired so much. Federico Oliver, author of *La Niña*, and a young poet, Luis Fernández Ardavín, propose from the columns of *El liberal* a tribute to the memory of the 'magical poet and master' of so many; Valle-Inclán, jealous of his priority in the cult, hastens to reply to them, with his characteristic vivacity, stating in the same paper that appropriate commissions are already functioning in all the American Republics, in France and Spain. This last—he says—'consists of D. Enrique Gómez Carrillo, D. Rufino Blanco Fombona, D. Pedro Emilio Coll, D. Amado Nervo and another writer, myself, though unworthy.' 'Without doubt', he adds, 'in naming me they were considering, rather than my merits, the memory I have of the poet, the admiration I feel for his work and the friendship I had with that *gran niño* during his life.' . . . In effect, Rubén Darío and Valle-Inclán pass together and united into literary history, creators in collaboration of a poetic style, in prose or verse, which not only brought Modernism into existence but also shapes directly or indirectly, in large measure, the language written afterwards: a language which later came, in the mere imitators, to be frankly mannerist (pp. 178–179)".

[18] Rubén Darío, "Historia de mis libros", *Obras completas*, I, p. 222. It is curious to note that years later in *Los cuernos de don Friolera*, Valle obviously recalls a verse of this composition to incorporate it in the dialogue between Don Manolito and Don Estrafalario. The latter says, in the theoretical conversation in the prologue to this work: "Sentimentalists who at bullfights suffer for the agony of the horses, are incapable of the aesthetic emotion of the contest: their sensibility becomes the same as equine sensibility and, by *unconscious cerebration* they assume for the bulls a fate like that of the disemboweled nags . . ."

[19] Rubén Darío, "Algunas notas sobre Valle Inclán", *Obras completas*, II, pp. 578–579.

[20] *Ibid.*, p. 579.

[21] Besides ";Aleluya!", a composition treated in the text, in the poem "*Clave V*", called "Bestiary", are to be found the following verses referring to the elephant: "Meditaciones eruditas / Que oyó Rubén alguna vez: / Letras sánscritas / Y problemas de ajedrez."

[22] In his lecture on "The Art of Writing", given in Buenos Aires in 1910, Valle refers to this composition of Darío's and quotes a stanza from it, saying: "No one understood better than Zorrilla that there are words and constructions that have prestige because of their Greek, Latin, Gothic or Arabic value. And as his equal can be placed only Rubén Darío, who knew how to unite words of remote ancestry with new words from foreign languages . . ." Francisco Madrid has collected the reviews of these lectures, printed in *La Nación. Op. cit.*, pp. 184–201.

[23] Alberto Ghiraldo, *El archivo de Rubén Darío* (Buenos Aires, 1943), pp. 419–421.

[24] Dictino Alvarez Hernández, *Op. cit.*, pp. 70–71, 136–137, and 187–190.

[25] Ghiraldo, *Op. cit.*, p. 419.

[26] Alvarez, *Op. cit.*, pp. 136–137.

27 Ghiraldo, *Op. cit.*, pp. 130–131.

28 Alvarez, *Op. cit.*, p. 137.

29 Ghiraldo, *Op. cit.*, pp. 420–421.

30 Alvarez, *Op. cit.*, p. 187.

31 Oliver Belmás, *Op. cit.*, p. 187.

32 Alvarez, *Op. cit.*, pp. 70–71.

33 We have already been concerned with this letter in an article entitled "Sobre la génesis de *Luces de bohemia*", (*Insula*, núms. 236–237, julio-agosto de 1966, p. 9) and, earlier, in some more extensive pages entitled "Las cartas de Valle Inclán a Rubén Darío" (*El Nacional*, núm. 1000, 29 de mayo de 1966). We have now seen that Guillermo Díaz-Plaja also has called attention to its importance in *Las estéticas de Valle Inclán* (Madrid, 1965), Nota 17, pp. 268–269.

34 We should like to mention here two significant works of Anthony N. Zahareas: "La desvalorización del sentido trágico en el esperpento de Valle-Inclán", *Insula* (núm. 203, octubre de 1963) and "The Esperpento and Aesthetics of Commitment", *Modern Languages Notes* (Vol. 81, núm. 2, marzo de 1966), pp. 159–173. Lastly, we have read the article of Gonzalo Sobejano, "*Luces de Bohemia*, elegía y sátira", *Papeles de Son Armadans*, IX (núm. 127, octubre de 1966), pp. 89–106.

35 Madrid, *Op. cit.*, p. 114.

36 In addition to the allusion to certain of Darío's poems ("Canción de otoño en primavera", "Peregrinaciones"), we are interested in showing here another direct quotation from the American poet inlaid in the dialogue of *Luces*. Dorio de Gádez (Escena cuarta) greets Max Estrella with words taken from the first verse of the "Responso" for Verlaine, saying: "Padre y maestro mágico, salud!"

37 Alvarez (*Op. cit.*, p. 198) reproduces a letter from Javier Bueno to Darío, dated March 9, 1912, with which he is sending the poet a eulogistic article by Valle. We do not know what text is meant.

38 In his book, already mentioned, about Valle, Díaz-Plaja anticipated us in listing some of the same thematic and verbal reminiscenses collected here. *Op. cit.*, pp. 259–270.

39 Arturo Marasso (*Rubén Darío y su creación poética* [La Plata, 1934], pp. 403–404), believes, for instance, that the archaisms of Darío's poem "Los motivos del lobo" come from the Galician writer's poetic drama *Voces de gesta*.

40 For this characteristic procedure of Valle's it is indispensable to consult pages of Alfonso Reyes ("Las fuentes de Valle Inclán", *Simpatías y diferencias* [México, 1945], II, pp. 60–61) and those of Amado Alonso ("Estructura de las *Sonatas* de Valle-Inclán", *Materia y forma en poesía* [Madrid, 1955], pp. 292–293).

41 In Valle's work there appears very frequently satire directed at the Academy and its members, but here we should like to mention only the burlesque portrait, presented in the *Farsa de la enamorada del Rey*, of the pompous and rhetorical Don Facundo (don Furibundo). Díaz-Plaja has seen in the aspect of this erudite personage unequivocal allusions to Julio Casares, recently, in 1919, elected to the Academy. *Op. cit.*, nota 28, p. 74.

42 Emma Susana Speratti Piñero, *La elaboración artística en Tirano Banderas* (México, 1957), pp. 12–39 and pp. 136–137. For Valle's sources Joseph H. Silverman's article is also important: "Valle-Inclán and Ciro Bayo," *NRFH*, XIV (núm. 1–2, 1960).

43 Emma Susana Speratti Piñero, "Génesis y evolución de *Sonata de otoño*," *RHM*,

XXV (núms. 1–2, enero-abril de 1959) pp. 57–80.

[44] Rubén Darío, "El modernismo," *Obras completas*, III, pp. 302–303.

We allow ourselves to cite here a judgment of Valle's about prose and verse, dating from 1934, which is interesting particularly for the allusion to Darío. Valle-Inclán, talking with Gerardo Diego, says: "There is no essential difference between prose and verse. Every good writer, like any good poet, will know how to find number, rhythm and quantity for his style. In this way great poets eliminate empty terms, *appoggiaturas*, inexpressive particles, and keep to noble words, full, plastic and extended. Thus Rubén Darío: 'Inclitas razas ubérrimas, sangre de Hispania fecunda,—espíritus fraternos, luminosas almas, ¡salve! . . .'" *Poesía española contemporánea* (Madrid, 1962), p. 85.

[45] The first to call attention to this verbal resemblance is César Barja ("Valle-Inclán," *Libros y autores contemporáneos* [Madrid, 1935], nota 7, p. 381), but the most interesting thing is to see how Valle is in love with this same image, re-elaborating it in various forms. We have noted the following examples: *Sonata de invierno* (Austral, 4a ed.), p. 104 and p. 149; *El resplandor de la hoguera* (Austral, 2a ed.) pp. 53, 117 and 123; and finally in *Tirano Banderas* Valle writes: " . . . encendían su roja llamarada las cornetas de los cuarteles."

[46] In "Marcha triunfal," these verses: "Los claros clarines de pronto levantan sus sones, / su canto sonoro / su cálido coro, / que envuelve en un trueno de oro / la augusta soberbia de los pabellones."

[47] Alonso Zamora Vicente has noted these and other examples of the contagion in his book *Las Sonatas de Ramón del Valle-Inclán* (Buenos Aires, 1951).

[48] For the genesis and elaboration of *Flor de santidad* this letter of Valle's is significant. In it he writes: "A few days ago I received a letter from you, here in this retreat of Aranjuez, when I came to write a novel five chapters of which I had had in hand for ten years. I finished it in twenty days . . . If I may be frank with you, this is the first time that I am in the least satisfied with my work. The title, *Flor de santidad*. It is a novel differing entirely in style and atmosphere and subject from the modern manner of writing novels. It resembles the books of the Bible rather than books of today; at other times it is Homeric, at others Gaelic . . ." *Indice*, IX (núms. 74–75, abril-mayo de 1954), p. 20.

[49] Raimundo Lida, "Cuentos de Rubén Darío," *Letras hispánicas* (México, 1958), pp. 233–234.

[50] Emma Susana Speratti Piñero, "Cómo nació y creció *El Ruedo Ibérico*," *Insula*, XXI (núms. 236–237, julio-agosto de 1966), p. 1 and p. 30.

[51] Darío wrote in "Los cisnes, I," a poem in *Cantos de vida y esperanza*: "Nos predican la fuerza con águilas feroces, / gerifaltes de antañ revienen a los puños . . ."

[52] In spite of a slight mechanical error, Díaz-Plaja has noted this same thematic trace, solely in respect to *El resplandor de la hoguera. Op. cit.*, p. 266, note 13.

[53] In an interesting work, perhaps still unpublished, which I have seen thanks to the author, Professor Gerard G. Flynn has compared "El palacio del sol," a story by Darío incorporated in *Azul . . .*, with Valle's *Cuento de abril*. Flynn finds gnostic traces in both works and concerns himself with the struggle between Christ and Cybele, pagan goddess of the earth, a struggle represented in *Cuento de abril* by the ascetic Infante de Castilla and the amorous princess Imberal de Provenza, azure country of art.

[54] Professor Sumner Greenfield has seen clearly the importance of this epoch in Valle-Inclán's trajectory, and has written about it as follows: "The most significant innovations of the period are found in the farces *La cabeza del dragón* and *La marquesa Rosalinda*—a new genre for Don Ramón. Here are shown numerous shifts of orientation that will change into important characteristics of post bellum *valleinclanesque* literature. Satire, parody and humor are now added to irony as *materia prima* of the style of Valle-Inclán. Stylization of the human figure, a vital aspect of his art in every period, turns for the first time extensively and systematically towards physical deformation through a variety of dehumanized forms, notable among them puppets and grotesque elements. It is worth noting, indeed, that these physical stylizations are employed here principally for their picturesque and humorous value and not with the incisive moral intention with which they will be used later. Various types of persons from earlier works also are found in transition, showing the way to the final development some ten years later (Don Juans, old dueñas, ladies in love, cuckolds), and incipient new types appear, anticipating in the same way Valleinclanesque future: ruffians, soldiers, pompous ministers of state and other members of court and government . . ." "Valle Inclán en transición: una brujería dialogada," *La Torre*, XIII, núm. 51, (septiembre-octubre de 1965,) p. 177.

[55] Díaz-Plaja, *op. cit.*, p. 225.

[56] The quoted reverberations of Darío in *Tirano Banderas* have been collected also by Professor Speratti in her book already mentioned, *La elaboración artística en Tirano Banderas*. For our own part we should like to point out how in *Farsa y licencia de la reina castiza* Valle seems to recall Rubén Darío in an openly ironic context. Referring to the grotesque Rey Consorte, already *animalizado*, Valle writes: "La vágula libélula de la sonrisa bulle / sobre su boca belfa, pintada de carmín," verses that echo, now with a sarcastic tone, others in Darío's "Sonatina." Perhaps it is worthwhile quoting here the final distich of "¡Aleluya!," the second *clave* of *La pipa de kif:* "Llevo mi verso a la Farándula: / Anímula, Vágula, Blándula."

[57] It is right to point out that the basis for these ideas is to be found in Ricardo Gullón, *Direcciones del modernismo* (Madrid, 1963), pp. 1–66, which, it is known, come from an immediate source, that is, Juan Ramón Jiménez, for whom Gullón has been and is chief literary executor.

[58] Juan Ramón Jiménez, *Retratos líricos* (Madrid, 1965), p. 43. My friend and colleague Miguel Enguídanos called my attention to this important text.

[59] Pedro Salinas, "Significación del esperpento o Valle Inclán, hijo pródigo del 98," *Literatura española. Siglo XX*, 2a ed. (México, 1949), p. 90.

[60] Rubén Darío, "Unamuno, poeta," *Obras completas*, II, p. 791.

[61] Quoted from the original text: "Modernismo," *La ilustración española y americana*, XLVI (núm. 7), 22 de febrero de 1902, p. 114.

[62] Octavio Paz believes that a basic sentiment in Modernist poetry is precisely "nostalgia for cosmic unity" and "its fascination with the plurality in which it is manifested." Paz, surprised that the Modernist poets have been taxed with being superficial, resumes his critical thought saying: "Modernism rises as an aesthetic of rhythm and flows into a rhythmic vision of the universe." "El caracol y la sirena (Rubén Darío)," *Cuadrivio* (México, 1965), pp. 28–29.

RUBÉN DARÍO

CANTOS

DE VIDA Y ESPERANZA

LOS CISNES Y OTROS POEMAS

MADRID

ARTURO TORRES-RIOSECO

RUBÉN DARÍO: CLASSIC POET

translated by David Flory

FROM HIS EARLIEST YOUTH,
Rubén Darío acquired the aura of an exceptional poet, one already
marked out for a singular and prodigious destiny. At first the indications were vague and superficial, as for example his precocious anti-
clericalism, his infantile Voltairianism and his predilection for scientific problems. Later on we have evidence of his extraordinary facility
for versification in his thirty-page poems, his improvisations on out-
landish subjects and his versified journalism. His prolific output attracted attention even in his native tropics, where indeed it became
confused with poetic genius. This mechanical facility for expression,
on its own, would not have taken him anywhere, but the young man
possessed a keen sensibility for the language, and little by little new
and poetic words began to appear in these long and prosaic compositions: new poetic words which were to be the first manifestations of
exoticism. When these efforts became more numerous, when the ex-
perimental linguistic process became more precise, the value of exoticism was defined in the mind of the writer. Each thread in this evo-
lutionary process signifies a great victory for the poet, after an intense
struggle, and the victory can sometimes be considered as a loss. In this
case the exoticism of Darío leads him (at least in appearances) to
hermeticism. Now hermeticism can take many forms: that of Góngora
and of Mallarmé, that of Hopkins, or that of Eliot and Pound. The
hermeticism of Darío, however, is more apparent than real, because
his genius is actually that of simplicity and clarity. Such apparent
hermeticism is due to a certain level of difficulty in understanding the
mythological vocabulary of Rubén. This relative unintelligibility is
the fault not of the poet, but of the reader, especially the ignorant and
proud reader. The man who today has a great respect for science and
praises Einstein without understanding his theory will not do the
same for a great painter, a great composer, or a great poet. All art that
he cannot understand is absurd and bad. The worst thing is that this
man does not *want* to understand; he stubbornly persists in his ig-
norance and his pride.

In the case of Darío's work the resulting incomprehension was absolute and revealed a general lack of culture. Poems like "A Verlaine"
were classified as incomprehensible. Stanzas such as the following
were regarded as extravagantly silly:

> Padre y maestro mágico, liróforo celeste
> que al instrumento olímpico y a la siringa agreste
> diste tu acento encantador.
> Panida, Pan tú mismo, que coros condujiste
> hacia el propíleo sacro que amaba tu alma triste
> al son del sistro y del tambor.

How easy it would have been to find words like *liróforo, siringa,
panida, propíleo, sistro* in a good dictionary! Can we wonder, however,
that an uninitiated reader reacted against these words when Don
Miguel de Unamuno himself made fun of the word "*siringa?*"

The entire concept of poetry evolved with Darío and not even his
best friends in Chile could understand him. Perhaps the only exception is Pedro Balmaceda, although the character of his prose work lent
itself less to stylistic evolution. One has only to cast a glance at the
major themes of Darío's contemporaries to see a pseudo-philosophical,
pseudo-religious, pseudo-political and pseudo-moral poetry, all without artistic plan, without aesthetic radiations. Rubén Darío was suffo-
cating in this prosaic atmosphere of practical goings-on, politics, vulgar
bohemia, tariffs, commercial enterprise and provincial journalism. He
was predestined to be the exemplary author of his time, the synthesizer
of a poetical language and an extremely refined artistic sensibility.
For that reason he escapes from the real world to the world of imagination and daydreams, to the world of poetry. This was the magic universe of the French Parnassians, especially of Théophile Gautier. Darío
began to create a new language, and this language, because of the lack
of Spanish and Chilean literary models and because of the poverty of
the language spoken in a society of incipient culture, was to be of a
classical-mythological type. It is true that this style may be only somewhat genuine, and even a sort of classical *pastiche,* but over the years,
as Darío matures, we see his style also acquiring the perfection of
mature classicism.

After *Azul* Darío tends to *perfection of form,* to *spiritual maturity,*
and to a *consciousness of the history of the Latin language.* It seems
there may have been a certain contradiction at this period between
the poet's eccentricity and his maturity, but later we see the fusion of

all the creative elements. Being a poet of Greco-Latin tradition, Darío possessed a mental equilibrium which restrained the romantic impulses of his youth and thus enabled correct Spanish syntax to predominate in his writings; his images have a Renaissance precision and harmony, and his symbols are most properly those of a high Mediterranean culture. The proof of what I am saying is that the vulnerable point of his style, the only thing that betrays a weakness, is his well-known use of Gallicisms, a minor element in the Modernist form.

The first centennial of the birth of Rubén Darío makes us pause to think for a moment of the significance of his work and of his life, because Darío has become a miracle, poetry incarnate. At first he was considered a precocious child-poet, then a daring reformer of the poetry of his time, still later the master of his generation of writers, and finally the major figure of Spanish-American lyric poetry. I think all these opinions are just. His precocity is proverbial. His power of innovation took him quickly from *Abrojos* to *Azul* and from *Azul* to *Prosas Profanas*. No one has denied him the title of leader of Modernism, and today he is unanimously recognized as the great poet of Spanish America. It is true that precocity is not an absolute sign of future greatness, but in this case the augury was fulfilled. His spirit of renovation could have run its course in mid-youth but it lasted until the end of his life. He synthesized the most profound qualities and characteristics of the movement which he initiated, and since 1916 his name has been held in the highest reverence.

Sometimes the glory of an artist derives from circumstances. Mysterious reasons accelerate or retard the growth of his fame. Rubén Darío is an example of true glory, based on the firm foundation of real values, which with the passage of time tend to become permanent, eternal.

Rubén Darío's life was simple. He did not create a courtly, luxurious, dramatic or heroic environment with which to surround himself. His loves were unfortunate; his love affairs, vulgar. Poverty was much more a reality to him than was opulence. The drama of his life developed in derisive forms. What could have been heroic became reduced to no more than empty gestures. His fame then grew on its own, as a result of those authentic values of artistic creation. He put it this way himself: "My poetry is mine within myself." (*mi poesía es mía en mí.*) And thus it was, always: an extremely personal combination, organic product coupled with mental elaboration. Some artists create an artificial atmosphere in order to exist within it, and thus detract from their personalities either by inventing something false or expressing their thoughts and their dreams in a language foreign to their own experience. What long hours of labor Góngora must have spent in raising the scaffolding of his *Soledades* and what nightmares Sor Juana must have had when composing her *Primero Sueño*! On the other hand the pure aesthetic joy of San Juan is authentic in his *Cántico Espiritual* as is that of Garcilaso in his *Eglogas*.

The stylistic evolution of Rubén Darío goes hand in hand with his ever-increasing mental profundity and with the enriching of his thematic materials. Although he must have felt the fever of violent imaginative outbursts, he restrained his impulses and established the equilibrium of his classically conceived work. Many times I have been tempted to make the analysis of the creative mind of Rubén Darío: the struggle between the vital passion and the philosophical serenity of the mature man. In this essay, we will discuss some isolated characteristics of his creative processes, starting with his *simplicity*, an essential part of his classical attitude.

In the year of his poetic initiation (1880) Darío showed that simplicity is the dominant characteristic of his art. In one of the first poems of this period, he writes:

> Las aves sus dulces trinos
> iban alegres cantando.
> Y blandamente saltando
> de rama en rama, en los pinos. . . .

And in one of the last, in 1915, he says:

> A Amy V. Miles
> dedico este tomo
> de versos galantes
> muy siglo XVIII.

Darío follows his first lyric attempts with anti-clerical poems; later comes his poetry on political and didactic topics which requires nothing of exotic attitudes or complex rhetoric. Around the age of sixteen, the courtly theme begins to dominate his poetry, and it seems that a period of more difficult and *recherché* technique was initiated, but this in fact is nothing more than an enriching of oriental vocabulary. Any dictionary could have solved the most abstruse linguistic problem for the timorous reader. This is the period in which he employs words such as *ámbar, hastchis, sándalo, loto, cinamomo,* the

period in which his poetic geography became enriched with *Golconda,*
Alejandría, Bassora, the period of adjectives such as *marfileño* and
ebúrneo, and yet a period in which his syntax retains its accustomed
simplicity. Among the most frequent influences on the Darío of those
days we note the names of Campoamor, Reina, Núñez de Arce,
Bécquer and Martí, none of whom was given to stylistic extravagances
of any kind.

Darío's desire for clarity is evident in the poem "La Poesía Caste-
llana" of 1882 in which he praises "simple, harmonious, lusty" poets,
condemns *culteranismo* and criticizes Góngora, who, he says,

> con las ondas de su ingenio
> antes tranquilo manantial de amores,
> derramó de su mente los fulgores
> de la española musa en proscenio.
>
> Mas ¡ay! la ruda tempestad del genio
> con sus horrendos rayos vibradores
> de su alma en el vergel, tronchó las flores
> que aromaron su dulce primigenio. . . .

which brings to mind the fact that years later he was to repeat the
same thought in a masterful way, in the poem "A los poetas risueños,"
from *Prosas Profanas:*

> prefiero vuestra risa sonora, vuestra musa
> risueña, vuestros versos perfumados de vino
> a los versos de sombra y a la canción confusa
> que opone el numen bárbaro al resplandor latino:
> y ante la fiera máscara de la fatal Medusa
> medrosa huye mi alondra de canto cristalino.

Around 1887 a desire for style (*voluntad de estilo*) manifests itself
in Darío. In *Azul* (1888) it is evident in the prose of his stories, and it
attracted the attention of the entire world. The fact that the simplicity
of the poems of *El año lírico* is maintained, indicates that essentially
the poet's talent seeks the most direct forms of expression, while the
prose writer is permitted the caprice of experimenting with new
elaborations of syntax, youthful artifices which do not complicate the
intention or disturb the measure of his composition. The novelty of
the prose of *Azul* is never based on mysterious complexities or strange
conceits. The verse (in the compositions added to the 1890 Guatemala
edition) becomes increasingly rich because of the vocabulary that

Darío was gathering along his poetic development and particularly because of the expert use of those words. Take, for example, his sonnet "Caupolicán." If we compare it with his "Central American" verses, we find an evident stylistic advancement. The harmonious quality of the composition is superior; the adjectives are chosen with exactness and propriety; the verses acquire a lightly symbolic sense; the historical references are more abundant. For the cultured reader there is no difficulty in understanding the meaning of the sonnet. In the remaining poems of this section the linguistic element livens the aesthetic, for example, in words such as *avatar, oarystis* and *cinegético*.

Darío arrived at the high point of his creative power in 1896, when his first great book, *Prosas Profanas*, appeared. His poetic language is now definitively formed. His inventions of syntax are unique in the history of Spanish literature; his vocabulary has a novelty and grace never before seen. It is not the formal syntactic richness of Góngora, mathematical and sometimes arbitrary, but rather a logical richness, with a sure movement toward excellence, with a high measure of reason, with the constant desire for perfection which always characterizes the work of the Nicaraguan poet. Darío had learned, assimilated, and improved. The superficially metaphoric became more profound and refined; it was transformed and became personal: "Most importantly, do not imitate anyone," declared the young master. With this, he created a cultured poetry of exemplary brilliance. And yet, he complained of the haste with which he wrote:

I have lacked the time and had too much weariness of heart and soul to make, like a good craftsman, my majuscules worthy of each page of the breviary. (*Prosas Profanas*)

Rubén penetrated this mythological artistic universe, assimilated it, and with his marvelous intuition turned it into something personal. In this way the ancient becomes modernized and that which was archeological is transformed into poetry.

In reviewing all the poems of *Prosas Profanas*, we find in "Era un aire suave," that marvelous example of euphony, of rhythmic grace, of word-discovery, such structural purity that at times a verse is composed of a simple succession of nouns, while at other times by a repetition of one verb in different forms. Some of the most famous poems of Rubén are included in this book: "Sonatina," a model of poetic ele-

gance, so ingenuously conceived
anthologies; "Margarita," in which today it appears in children's
to the intensity of passion; "Heraldos, florescence of form gives way
deciphered in natural form; "Coloquio which a chain of symbols is
philosophical explanation of the myth o s Centauros," a simple yet
en Gris Mayor," which presents a large qu divine beasts, "Sinfonía
images, difficult to interpret. In "El Reino Int ity of new and strange
of his most beautiful allegories, in a perfect, tra r" Darío offers us one
ture. arent, classic struc-

It might be observed that Darío still favors the na
story-in-verse, which does not lend itself to the subt ive form, the
style. In "Recreaciones arqueológicas" the greater or l tillation of
for comprehension corresponds once again to the proportio capacity
culture of the reader. This is due as much to the cultural geo literary
the poems as to their symbolism. It is apparent that Darío was hy of
with René Ménard's *Mythologie dans l'art ancien et moderne* (iar
and that this book had a great influence on his style. To the knowl
of the Greek world through its poets, we must add what Darío obtain
from the plastic arts, the painting of vases and bas-reliefs transmuted
into lyric beauty by the words of the young poet.

In *Cantos de Vida y Esperanza* (1905) we find explicit statements
concerning his manner of feeling and executing beauty. Everything
within him is "anxiety, ardor, pure sensation and natural vigor"; there
is in him no "falsehood, or make-believe, or literature." His soul is the
essence of sincerity. There are in this work poems of such marvelous
precision and simplicity, that Darío convinces us that this is indeed his
most genuine creative vein. Consider, for example, "La dulzura del
ángelus," "Canción de otoño en primavera," "Letanía de nuestro señor
Don Quijote," "Lo fatal," and many others. In the *Cantos* there are
tortured verses, philosophical verses, sensual and mystic verses, but
there are never abstruse or *conceptista* verses. He sometimes comes in
contact with Góngora, but he never lets himself be seduced by him. It
seems that his own poetical profundity kept him away from a poetic
structure which was more brilliant, but which was also of limited dur-
ation and vitality.

In his "Dilucidaciones" (explanatory writings) in *El Canto Errante*
(1907), Rubén affirms his belief in sincerity and simplicity, and continues to put it into practice. He buries himself in his interior world,

life, the accelerated anarchy of his
he contemplates the mysteries‚sophical attitude. His style, however,
day, and he develops a more ⁄
is always careful and exact‚culminates in *Poema de Otoño* (1910), a
And so Darío's poetic‚piest artistic expression of the poet, his de-
poem of synthesis, the‚n, in which we see life, in perfect harmony,
finitive philosophy of‚ity:
in all its purity and

> Y sentimos la vida pura,
> clara, real,
> cuando la envuelve la dulzura
> primaveral.

ɔ had suffered; who had written once of anguish in lines
A man‚ɔue no hay dolor más grande que el dolor de ser vivo" (there
such ‚eater pain than the pain of being alive); "La camisa de mil
is ‚sangrientas," (the shirt of a thousand bloodstained thorns); "La
‚á es triste, amarga, y pesa" (life is sad, bitter, hard to bear); says
‚ere—facing the moment of truth, and affirming the exaltation of the
individual:

> Gozad del sol, de la pagana
> luz de sus fuegos;
> gozad del sol, porque mañana
> estaréis ciegos.
>
> En nosotros la vida vierte
> fuerza y calor.
> Vamos al reino de la muerte
> ¡por el camino del Amor!

Even though many of the poems written after 1910 are of great human significance and philosophical inspiration, in which the thought of death makes the poet's voice tremble, it would be futile to look through them for "reconditeness," for the obscurity, or for the metaphysical orientation of other poets. Quite the contrary, Darío's last poem, "Divagaciones," shows us that his trajectory was unswerving:

> Mis ojos espantos han visto,
> tal ha sido mi triste suerte;
> cual la de mi Señor Jesucristo
> mi alma está triste hasta la muerte.
>
> Hombre malvado y hombre listo
> en mi enemigo se convierte;

> cual la de mi Señor Jesucristo
> mi alma está triste hasta la muerte.

The first poetic attempts of Rubén were imitative of the prosaic Campoamor (with a youthful and playful "bad taste") or of the exaggerated sentimentality of Bécquer's disciples or of the pseudophilosophical tirades of Núñez de Arce, and they persist thus until his arrival in Chile. Shortly thereafter, the Parnassian note is sounded, first in prose and then in poetic anticipation of *Azul*. His pure literary taste still predominates; sophisticated French models replace old Spanish mentors.

But soon uncomprehending critics began to protest. Valera himself, basically fair in his study of Rubén dwelt at too great a length on his "mental gallicism"; Clarín (Leopoldo Alas) revealed his inability to understand contemporary poetic techniques; later Unamuno did not seem to realize the transcendental value of the renovation that was taking place in Spanish literary style.

Darío, then, turns out to be a strange poet to those used to traditional Spanish poetry, and a misfit of a poet, surrounded by the versifiers of America, who were busy singing the praises of political "caudillos," celebrating the beauty of the wives of presidents, deifying ministers and dissatisfied patrons. These versifiers, who were the first to applaud Darío's early compositions on themes such as those just mentioned, were also the ones who later began to give him a reputation as a difficult poet. His literary enemies were of three kinds: the masters of traditional taste, those who confused poetry with patriotism, who accepted a single artistic norm; the writers who envied him because they feared that Darío's triumph would end their local success, and finally, the ignorant poetasters for whom poetry was merely a social activity.

We can be thankful that Darío understood his mission, that he knew how to liberate himself from his initial literary environment, from the mediocrity of his friends and protectors, and from the vulgar bohemia that could have destroyed him. This is what he understood and said in his great poem "Yo soy aquél":

> Mi intelecto libré de pensar bajo,
> bañó el agua castalia el alma mía,
> peregrinó mi corazón y trajo
> de la sagrada selva la armonía.

Today those to whom mythology and its vocabulary are unknown,

whose knowledge of poetry is strictly limited, still speak of the compli-
cated genius of the Nicaraguan poet. A basic lesson in good taste and
a dictionary would be sufficient to show them their error.

I have tried to show that Rubén Darío is a classic poet, and I believe
that he is just that. I see in him a case analogous to that of Lope de
Vega, who, dazzled by the genius of Góngora, imitated him only to
return to his own original simplicity. In the same way Darío imitated
brilliant poets (although they were inferior to him) and later returned
to his candor, to his sincerity, to his clear interpretation of the world
and to his simple and perfect form.

Darío now ranks on the highest artistic level beside Garcilaso,
because of his lyrical fluidity and his immense tenderness; beside San
Juan de la Cruz, because of the psychological mastery with which he
handles the poetic idiom; beside Quevedo, because of rigorous structure and formal perfection; beside Fray Luis de León, because of his
serenity. In spite of the fact that the famous verses of Darío

> Amo más que la Grecia de los griegos
> La Grecia de la Francia, porque en Francia . . .
>
> Demuestran más encantos y perfidias
> las diosas de Clodión que las de Fidias . . .
>
> Verlaine es más que Sócrates y Arsenio
> Houssaye supera al viejo Anacreonte

seem to express a definitive predilection for modern French culture
over the classical culture of the ancients, Vergil and Ovid dominate
Rubén's aesthetic horizon during the epoch of *Prosas Profanas*, and
Platonic sentiment is the essence of his feeling in the love poems. In all
the work of the great Nicaraguan poet the intensity of his sense of
classical beauty gives way only to the intensity of his fear of death.

OTOÑO

Los versos de Hugo, el son de flauta elegíaco de Millevoye, un grabado en madera de Narts, todas estas cosas y otras más surgie, ron en mi imaginación, como evocadas, delante de la palabra negra sobre la página blanca: *Otoño....*; pero más que todo, fuiste tú, Belisa, la que surgiste cual de una cripta, de mi alma, desolada bajo una lluvia de hojas pálidas, á la hora en que, después de mediodía, la tarde otoñal mira melancólicamente hacia el lado en que aparece el primer lucero de la noche. Porque tú simbolizas para mí la estación de la melancolía en que los árboles quedan sin las galas de su juventud y la fruta que no se ha cortado á tiempo cae y se pudre. ¿Recuerdas? Juntos nacimos á la vida, y la primavera nos saludó coronándonos de sendas coronas floridas. Nos criaron de modo que bien pudimos, al amor del trópico, en aquel país de fuego, jugar eficazmente á Pablo y Virginia. Fuiste tú la que por primera vez despertaste con la frescura floral y carnal de tu cuerpo maravilloso, la llama dormida de mi sangre ; y tus ojos azules, fijos en los míos, en el tiempo de nuestras dos adolescencias, y la roja calor de cuando en cuando empurpuraba tus mejillas, y la palpitación columbina de tu naciente seno, me revelaban que en ti también nacía la gracia misteriosa del deseo. Ese era el momento, Belisa, ése era el instante sagrado ; pero no supimos tender la mano y cortar la rosa. La manzana quedó en el árbol y la primavera pasó, con su cortejo pomposo. Yo partí á lejanos países, pues mi alma de Simbad tiende á buscar siempre horizontes y paisajes nuevos, así fuese fuera del mundo : *anywhere out of the world....* ; pero en todos lugares, desde aquellos días de llamas, cuando el sueño me conduce á su imperio, he ahí que tú apareces tal con el encanto de tu dominadora hermosura sensual ; y tú eras la amada, la querida de los ensueños. Lo eres aún. Pues aunque te haya vuelto á ver, vestida de negro, simbólica imagen del otoño, marchita ya bajo tu rubia cabellera, gastada, ajada, semejante á un árbol que deja caer sus hojas de oro enfermo, en el mundo de los ensueños renaces intacta para el deseo. Las rosas de tu rostro son las mismas ; tu perfume es el mismo ; tus labios, tus senos, son los mismos ; y así, en una rabia de amor, caes bajo la tiranía de mis besos, bajo la locura de mis caricias. Y es porque, ¡ oh Belisa, triste imagen otoñal ! el deseo que no tuvo en sus labios la copa ardientemente aspirada, quedó en el fondo de mi alma, en donde, al amparo de la noche y del sueño, me rehace una adolescencia, y del real otoño, de la lamentación de las hojas caídas y de la tristeza del árbol marchito, forma una alegría de abril, un canto de gracia erótica, una primavera, que, como la del supremo Sandro, va tejiendo guirnaldas, rítmica, en un paso armonioso *incensu patuit Dea*.

RUBÉN DARÍO.

[A contribution of Rubén Darío to *Caras y Caretas*, Buenos Aires.]

ENRIQUE ANDERSON-IMBERT

RUBÉN DARÍO AND THE FANTASTIC ELEMENT IN LITERATURE

translated by Anne Bonner

I TRUST MY READERS WILL ALLOW me to start from the premise that literature is, ultimately, a means of escape from reality; not only from the physical reality around us but also from our own psychic reality that overwhelms us with emotions, impulses and ideas. The writer discovers that certain very personal experiences provide him with a peculiar esthetic delight. What interests him as a source of creativity is not reality but rather this new revelation, whose value is primarily artistic. He has moved reality into the distance leaving a void which, in turn, is filled by an image wrapped in symbols. It is as if in the space left behind, a figure had come forth and said: "Here I am" (literally "I appear"), which is precisely what the word *phantasia* means in Greek.

To the extent it replaces a reality already moved aside, all literature is fantastic. But even so, there is some fiction that is especially concerned with creating believable yet autonomous worlds. This is the case in fantastic literature. With the power of his imagination, the writer renders helpless the norms that had ruled our minds before, suggesting instead the possibility of other norms as yet unknown.

Among the various types of stories Rubén Darío wrote,[1] there were some that fit this description of "fantastic" or supernatural tales based on mystical experiences, on dreams, on states of mind bordering on insanity. These metaphysical, metapsychical, mythological, allegorical stories, fairy tales and lives of saints tell of imaginary happenings Darío did not always invent. But even when he chose to work with actual occurrences, he would either make them unbelievable, disfigure them with extravagant interpretations, or otherwise alter them by providing a mysterious setting. Somehow his use of language enabled him to dislodge events from the hold of empirical reality, elevating them to the realm of fantasy. Through his skillful selection of words, his choice of rhythms appropriate to the movement of his lyrical metaphors, the use of synesthesia and the transposition of techniques from music and the plastic arts, Darío managed to "unrealize" reality.[2]

The verbal texture of a story helps to intensify the symbolic transformation of facts. In addition, a story is composed of certain structural elements: the more form given by such elements, the more the work distinguishes itself from reality which is amorphous. The writer's imagination is not only evident in his stylistic traits, but also on higher levels; in ideas that emanate from the text and register with our minds and our memories. There is form to be found, for example, in the way action is woven into a plot and given a certain design.[3] There is also form in narrative sequence,[4] in points of view,[5] in interior duplication,[6] in the utilization of other literary genres within the story.[7] For the present I will be concerned with only one of these structural elements: the surprise ending. This particular device can make any given narrative situation, no matter how realistic, seem the contrary. Life is, of course, full of surprises, but they follow no plan. In a story, however, unexpected turns imply a strategy of deliberate concealment. Darío keeps us deceived so he can shock us with his ending. He does this often[8] but, in my mind, the two best examples are "Un sermón" and "Respecto a Horacio." The device is even more effective because in both stories the author is playing boldly with the element of time.

As Darío wrote "Un sermón" in 1892, he projected himself into the future and, from that imaginary point of time, evoked a scene that supposedly took place the first day of January, 1900. This is a paradoxical resurrection: not of the past, but of the future. With verbs in the past tense Darío pretends to record the sermon he said he heard Fray Pablo deliver in St. Peter's basilica at the inauguration of the twentieth century, a term which for Darío and his readers involved a vague conception of future time. There is yet another surprise.

Upon leaving, still under the magic spell cast by the monk's sermon, I inquired of a French journalist who was assigned to the event:
"Who is that great man? Why, he's another St. John Chrysostom!"
"As you probably know," he replied, "this is his first sermon. He's almost seventy and was born in Spain. His name is Fray Pablo de la Anunciación and he is one of the true geniuses of the 19th century. His secular name was Emilio Castelar."

The shock of discovering, in a story written in 1892, this anachronistic apostasy that in 1900 the impetuous liberal, Emilio Castelar, will become a monk (or *has* become a monk, if we adopt the narrator's point of view) was strengthened even more by a coincidence Darío did not count on. As it turned out, that same Castelar whom we see in a fictional 1900 in the mysterious habit of an Augustinian monk, had actually died in 1899. If to begin with, his story had been just a playful joke, afterward Darío must have felt that it had been some kind of a premonition.

In "Respecto a Horacio" Darío set a trap that goes off only if the reader is familiar with Horace's Ode XIII, Book II. The slave, Lucio Galo, had confessed (in writing) that out of resentment, he had arranged for a tree to fall and crush Horace. Five years later, Galo adds a few lines to his confession: he is pleased with his criminal attempt because as Horace barely escaped the tree falling toward him he was able to write "the beautiful verses that begin: *ille et nefasto te posuit die. . . .*" Darío's text ends here but the reader who knows that once a tree actually did fall on Horace and almost killed him, is left with the remaining lines of the ode echoing in his mind. It is as if Horace himself were continuing the narration with his own words:

> On an ill-omened day, accursed tree,
> Did your first planter plant you, and profane
> The hand that reared you to the infamy
> Of country-side, and to descendants' bane.[9]

If the style used to transform language into poetry together with the structural forms that make up a story in themselves are able to attenuate real anecdotes, it is clear their effect will be even more powerful on material which, to begin with, is unreal.

What does it mean to say that certain material for a story is "unreal?" This is surely the most difficult problem in the analysis of fantastic literature.

The material for any narration is traditional in the sense that the number of possible situations is, of course, very limited and the writer has no choice but to repeat them. It is interesting to see what Darío did with old themes and, more important, what he felt to be the fantastic as opposed to the "real" elements in each one of them. Just as in the most realistic story the narrator's fantasy intervenes, in the most unrealistic narration there will always be a minimum of reality.

We have seen that a fantastic story rejects empirical reality to put in its place the image of a reality freed from psychological and physical laws. Obviously this freedom cannot be complete. If the work were to obey restrictions imposed on the real world it would no longer be literature. But if it could totally escape psychological and physical nature it would cease to be intelligible. Invention will always build upon realistic elements. So it is that the critic is first tempted to distinguish fantastic literature on the basis of its subject-matter; he would measure the angle of deviation between the content of a story and reality as we know it, setting up categories ranging from the probable to the possible, from the possible to the improbable, from the improbable to the impossible.

According to these divisions, there would be stories with probable situations like "El fardo." A man is crushed to death while unloading a ship on a wharf in Chile. Any insurance salesman could calculate the possibilities of such an accident on the job. There would be stories with possible situations like, for example, "La ninfa." At a party given by an actress in her mansion, a poet dares to doubt the existence of nymphs. The following day as he is walking through the park, the actress appears before him naked: now he knows he has seen a nymph. Although it may not seem probable that a hostess would undress for her guests, still it is possible. So much so, in fact, that years after having written this story (1887) something very similar happened to Darío himself. While in Hamburg in 1911, he and Fabio Fiallo paid a visit to a distinguished woman who was known to entertain prominent artists and writers in her salon. That afternoon the three of them were alone. Darío and Fiallo recited poetry. Their hostess, out of sheer gratitude, undressed and allowed the men to admire her beauty. Darío was convinced he had seen a nymph.[10]

"La muerte de Salomé" would be classified as an improbable story, although Darío presents it as an historical document. It is, however, improbable that Salome's head, severed by a gold serpent she wore at her neck, would have rolled next to John the Baptist's, which she herself had had cut off shortly before.

The events of "La pesca" would be labeled impossible. The chances that a fisherman, having thrown his nets into the sea where the stars were reflected, could catch the planet Saturn, and that his son could eat the star, then play with its huge rings as with the bones of a fish are, I believe, not very good.

Obviously this method of tabulating the realistic elements of a story is not valid. If such things can be measured and weighed it is because they are no longer in the story, but only in the mind of the critic. The temptation, then, to arrange stories along a probability scale should be resisted. Such scientific classification is not compatible with literature. The critic's criterion should be literary: not to focus on the nature of things, but rather on their function. After all, the same applies to the short story as to the metaphor. One might ask if a metaphor is new and alive or if it has been used over and again, if it has been fossilized in the language and reduced to a cliché. To answer this question we have to consider whether the speaker was conscious of having united two logical meanings in a lyrical synthesis. In the same way we ask if a fantastic story is new. Do the things related in it, however absurd, pass for the truth? Again we must discern whether or not the metaphor was aware of referring to a dual reality. What the author does is to establish tangential contact between a reality common to all men and an extremely personal reality of his own. Once there on the faint border line between two worlds, does he distinguish what exists only for him and what also exists for the rest of us? We can say that a story is fantastic if it can be substantiated from the text that the author's intention is to credit as the only explanation for the events he narrates, the one he himself has chosen to give. This explanation can be arbitrary and independent of rational causes that might apply to analogous situations outside of fiction. To study Darío's fantastic stories we must first understand what his intention was.

When I speak of intention, of course, I am not referring to the psychological motivation of Darío the man. This does not concern the critic and, even if it did, he could not pretend to psychoanalyze his subject. He should limit himself to the artistic intention of the author such as it is expressed in each story. When dealing with truly great writers, it is easy enough to put aside consideration of psychological experience and dedicate oneself instead to the description and evaluation of the work. But Darío, a pure poet, was impure as a writer of short stories. His fantastic tales are so much colored by obscure emotions that we cannot help but relate them to personal psychological sources beginning with his first disquieting experiences as a child.

Fears arising from superstition, beliefs imparted by the Church, repeated readings of *A Thousand and One Nights*, ghost stories, horror novels: all these left an indelible mark on an already nervous and impressionable Darío. For a short time as an adolescent, he demonstrated anti-clerical attitudes, but almost immediately came back to the Church; at least, that is, he declared himself respectful toward her mysteries and sacraments. He did not, however, take part in the rituals or the moral teachings of Catholicism. From 1890 on he professed a kind of religious syncretism that combined and confused bits of Catholic theology with oriental cosmogonies, the cabala with Masonry, the theories of Pythagoras with mesmerism, and esoteric doctrines with the occult sciences. At this same time, he was introduced to theosophy and the books of Madame H. P. Blavatsky, among others.

When he wrote stories of fantasy, Darío let himself be influenced by these beliefs. He would tell of things that had no logical explanation, that could not be substantiated by the natural sciences, but that, nonetheless, he believed took place. He seemed to be stimulated by the kind of literature that emphasized the improbable or even the impossible. Such writing has a long tradition. It was known to Antiquity, to the Middle Ages and to the Renaissance. But the history of fantastic literature, as we understand it today, dates back only to the end of the 18th century. After the Industrial Revolution, the critical scientific mind discarded the old phantasms and turned to the art of inventing new ones. Like Coleridge said, one had to "procure for these shadows of imagination that willing suspension of disbelief which constitutes poetic faith."[11] At the same time the new critical spirit was provoking a reaction, a return to the oriental, medieval tradition. There was a little of everything: skeptical writers who amused themselves with extravagant notions, fanatics taken in by the supernatural, etc. From it all a new kind of story was emerging; a story designed to excite the reader with its atmosphere of terror and suspense and to shock him with an unexpected ending. It was this fantastic literature, a product of the period during the 19th century between Romanticism and Symbolism, that Darío saw subsumed and given new life.

The relationship between Darío's vague religiosity and his also vague symbolism can be documented. His initiation into theosophy in 1890 had an immediate effect on stories written during the same period. Between 1893 and 1894, he not only wrote the majority of his stories, but in them appear his most novel thematic content: mysteries, magic, miracles, ghosts, psychic anomalies, and experiments in time. Two of his essays, both published in Buenos Aires, are helpful as clues to the influence that theosophy and so-called decadent literature had on the material of these stories. In "Onofroffismo: La comedia psíquica" (1895), he speaks of the poetic inspiration he got from his readings in theosophy. He says that in spite of the well-founded attacks against the "psychic comedy" of the theosophists and occultists, he, Darío, because of his credulity as a poet and his fondness for the supernatural, continues to believe, at least, as long as "he does not leave the realm of his dreams," in the "magical powers of a Madame Blavatsky," "surrounded by her subjects like the queen of a fairy tale." In the essay on "Richard Le Gallienne," we find his conviction that literary symbolism was an invitation to tales of mystery:[12]

The so-called decadents . . . have searched everywhere for deep manifestations of the world-soul. They have found in Eastern cultures a world of exotic practices . . . They have removed all obstacles from the way of the psyche . . . Who better than Poe and his followers has explored the dark realm of Death?

Interestingly, Darío calls Poe the father of the decadents. The fascination the French symbolists felt for him is, of course, well-known. There were also other important names in the formation of Darío, the story writer, but since this is not the place to go into them all,[13] I would like to examine the case of Poe because it is especially revealing. In Darío's attitude toward this writer we find the key for understanding his artistic intent.

In his chapter on Poe in *Los Raros*, Darío expressed amazement that one who had created such strange worlds had not been a believer: "Philosophical speculation stood between him and the faith he should have had as a great poet. . . . He did not believe in the supernatural." It did not occur to Darío that perhaps the strangeness of the world envisioned by Poe may have benefited from that very philosophical detachment with respect to his fantasies. Poe was, in fact, a declared materialist. He reduced the psychic to the physical; for him spirituality was either material or it did not exist. The supernatural element in his stories was gratuitous; the note of gloom was owing more to a morbid curiosity about death than to religious or metaphysical concepts of reality. If Darío was surprised to find that Poe was imaginative at the same time that he was skeptic, it was because in his own case imagination was inseparable from religious beliefs. Darío found metaphysical concepts in "Mesmeric Revelation" but he apparently did not know that in "Marginalia," Poe had mocked the Swedenborgians who took him seriously: "This story," he had said, "is a pure fiction from beginning to end."

In an article on H. G. Wells,[14] Darío seems to contradict what he had said with respect to Poe, though here again his reasoning betrays the same desire to associate whims of fantasy with magical explanations. If before he found it hard to believe that Poe should write "extraterrestrial fantasies" in spite of his skepticism, now he assumes

that Wells' "extraordinary fantasies" are in some way involved with
the occult sciences. He is seemingly unwilling to accept that these
writers, famous for their imaginations, would invent situations they
did not believe in. His comments on "The Plattner Story" are typical.
Mr. Plattner, a chemist, is hurled from the earth by an explosion and
returns days later with his anatomy reversed: his heart on the right
side, etc. In 1897 Wells was sophistically playing with physical-
mathematical speculations on the plurality of spatial dimensions. Confronted with this example of science-fiction, Darío does not stop to consider Wells' mischief in speaking of something so strange as if it were
an ordinary occurrence. Instead he takes seriously what, in the story,
is nothing more than a possible hallucination of the protagonist: that
Plattner says he saw dead people watching over us in outer space. In
spite of the fact that Wells was an atheist and did not believe in life
after death, or in the transmigration of the soul, Darío, rather than
include him among the physical-mathematicians, considers him a
spiritualist like Annie Bessant:

"The Plattner Story" takes on a level which undoubtedly enhanced the
author's particular talent. I mean the hereafter, the other life, whatever
conscious part remains of the human being after death . . . It would seem
that Wells was either a member of select groups or a successful researcher
of occult practices. This would not be surprising in the land of Annie
Bessant, so often visited by Hindu theologians and masters of the occult.

Apparently what motivated Darío in the writing of certain fantastic
stories was a very personal combination of psychological forces—
superstition, anxiety about the mysterious, fear of death—the same
forces operative in his verse as well. In some of his stories the unbelievable occurrences stemmed from non-artistic preoccupations. Instead of contemplating the figures of his imagination at a suitable
distance, that is, from an esthetic perspective, Darío was unable to
separate them from his own feelings. In this sense we can say that
his belief in the supernatural, after inciting his imagination, deterred
it and forbid it to go any farther. It was both a stimulus and an
obstruction.

Darío's success or lack of it in the fantastic genre depends on
whether or not he can liberate himself from theology, theosophy,
oneiromancy and occultism. Such "liberation" does not mean his
"ceasing to believe" but only his being able to see those beliefs in an
esthetic light and to understand that they cannot be valid as true

explanations but merely as incitement to artistic creation. Religion, as a system of beliefs established by a church and accepted by a community, does not always allow for the free play of imagination. Fantasy is more effective artistically the more it risks caprice, even heresy. Let us compare two of Darío's religious allegories that take place during the life of Christ.

The first is conventional: "Historia prodigiosa de la princesa Psiquia." Psiquia, the soul, is unhappy because she cannot be satisfied possessing love, or glory, or strength, or science but only the secret of Death. When the resuscitated Lazarus whispers this secret in her ear, she falls into eternal sleep.

The other allegory, "Las tres Reinas Magas," is the Christ story with the sexes changed. The one who is born in a manger is Crista, the daughter of a virgin and a worker. Three queens visit her and offer her the choice—after her martyrdom on the cross—of one of three paradises. Crista, who is a symbol of the poet's soul, chooses the paradise of myrrh.

This is the land of woman; the land where marvelous feminine flesh, displayed in its pagan, natural nudity casts a rosy hue upon the trembling twilights. Under the azure canopy turtledoves fly, and now and then the green thickets reveal flitting white shapes pursued by hairy creatures with cleft hooves.

In my opinion, the story of a Psiquia who longs to unveil the mystery of death and does so only by dying herself, since it does not avoid the commonplace, is artistically weak. On the other hand, the story of a female Christ who prefers a paradise of satyrs is so unexpected that it frees itself from the religious theme and, once outside the reach of orthodoxy, soars freely.

Darío's stories of miracles further demonstrate that fantasy suffers when not divorced from religious belief. The fantastic element here is not the miraculous event itself, but the way in which it is presented. Someone can tell of a miracle that upset the entire natural order of the universe without exciting our imaginations in the least. If the reader is a believer, theological explanations have influenced him beforehand and save him from that perplexed state so familiar to devotés of fantastic literature.

In "Cuento de Noche Buena," a monk goes back in time so that he is present at the birth of Christ. While he is adoring the Child, the organ he used to play in his monastery rings out with celestial music.

The material was most fitting for a fantastic tale: two occurrences—the friar's adoration and the music from his organ—separated by centuries and yet simultaneous! But Darío, more religious than imaginative, preferred to give to his work the tone of an ordinary hagiography rather than present in a flash the paradox of time and eternity.

In another of these stories, there is a monk who practices the occult sciences. With a camera given him by the Devil, he photographs Christ's face in the sacred host. The first version (1896) was called "Verónica," the second (1913) "La extraña muerte de fray Pedro." An excessive religious piety in his last years affected Darío in such a way that his artistic liberty suffered. In the 1896 version, Christ, surprised by the click of the shutter, naturally appears in the picture with a horrified expression: *Terrible*, says Darío. By 1913, the look, unfortunately, from an esthetic point of view, has become sweet. Obviously Darío, more attentive to the conventions of a religious tale than to the demands of a fantastic one, forgot that, if there are looks that kill, the one that killed Fray Pedro must have been "terrible," not sweet. He thought more of the image of the smiling Christ children carry engraved on their medallions than of the image of a Christ who intimidates us from atop Byzantine altars. The first title was also better: "Verónica," the name of the Roman woman who wiped Christ's bleeding face and carried away its imprint on her cloth, was an ingenious if not somewhat irreverent title for the photograph.

In short, a miracle excites our imaginations the more distant it is, not only from the natural laws governing reality but also from the conventions of a cosmogony founded on the supernatural.

The same is true of the dreams Darío used in some of his stories. He also believed in oneiromancy. In a group of articles written in 1911—collected after his death and entitled *El mundo de los sueños*—Darío said that for him dreams were not merely a psychological phenomenon but that they represented a supernatural reality. "There is much truth," he added, "to the ancient belief among occultists that everything we imagine, no matter how marvelous and strange, does exist." This idea that dream-images correspond to real things entered into the composition of some of Darío's stories. To see just how this happened, let us look at the genesis of "La larva."

For a time, Darío was obsessed with a nightmare in which he saw a cadaver coming toward him. During the discussion of a macabre painting by Gauguin in an article included in *Los raros* ("Rachilde"), he alluded to this dream without revealing that it was his own.

. . . the experience elicited by nightmares in which walking corpses approach the dreamer, touch him, embrace him and, in spite of being only a dream, he actually feels the contact of waxen skin and perceives the peculiar and frightful odor of dead flesh.

But elsewhere—in *El mundo de los sueños*—he does claim the dream.

I cannot find a way to describe the sensation I have in dreams when *something*, an unknown being who in that realm of darkness takes the shape of a spectre, a human-like monster, or a walking corpse touches me, takes my hand or simply brushes past me. There are countless descriptions that come to mind. It is something like an electric shock, at once painful and horrifying. But it is more than that. It is something that I just cannot put into words.

In *La vida de Rubén Darío escrita por él mismo* (1912), he makes a slip that is very significant to our knowledge about the evolution of the story "La larva." Inadvertently Darío repeats the same scene: once as a nightmare brought on by nervous tension and again as a true supernatural apparition. In chapter IX, he remembers his first frightening dream when he was 14 years old:

I had a dream in which I sat reading near a table at home, by the light of a kerosene lamp . . . In the dark frame of the door I saw a whitish shape like that of a human being wrapped in linen cloth. I became terror-stricken because I noticed that it moved toward me without walking . . . I felt utterly helpless as "the thing" came near me. I tried to run but I could not move. And the sepulchral materialization came closer, filling me with such indescribable fear that my whole body was paralized. That thing had no face and yet it had a human body. That thing had no arms and yet I knew it was going to embrace me. That thing had no feet and yet it was already close to me. Then came my greatest horror—the hideous odor of dead flesh. Something like an arm touched me, and I felt shocked as if by electricity. Realizing that I had to defend myself, I bit the "thing" and it was exactly as if I had sunk my teeth into a candle of oil wax. Then I woke up sweating and with a feeling of dread.

In chapter XLVI, recalling that same year of his youth, what was a nightmare in chapter IX is a real experience:

. . . one night just before dawn, in the square in front of the cathedral of León, Nicaragua, while in complete possession of my senses, I saw and touched a larva, a horrible sepulchral materialization.

Why is it that Darío would confuse dreams with fantasies? Like the theosophists, he seemed convinced that everything he saw really existed. A person who is sleeping, drunk or delirious may not have the control of a medium, theosophists conceded, but because his mind is relaxed he is susceptible to "waves of Astral Light." So it was that Darío believed the larvae and pupae he saw in his dreams were real. In *Viaje a Nicaragua* (1909), he said:

When I was 14, in front of the cathedral I saw a larva, or what the theosophists call an elemental. What I saw was true and really there. However, I will not insist upon it, for I'm afraid that my wise friend José Ingenieros might become interested in the account and look upon it as those who deal with science and have no faith look upon such matters.

"La larva" was published the following year in *Caras y Caretas*. The narrator, Isaac Codomano—an obvious Hebrew-Persian pseudonym for Rubén Darío, also a Hebrew-Persian name—swears he saw the larva:

The shape turned toward me and uncovered its face. Horror of horrors! The face was viscous and decomposed; one eye hung over a bony and oozy cheek. Then I perceived the smell of putrefaction.

What these quotes indicate is that, in the genesis of "La larva," there was non-literary interference. A recurring nightmare, reinforced by theosophical beliefs, became a story the author tried to pass off not as a fantastic creation but as an autobiographical document. In "La larva" Darío let himself become involved with his own beliefs. On other occasions he was able to escape them.

In "Thanathopía" (1893), the first in this series of macabre tales, the vision of a walking cadaver was the product of pure imagination. A magician's son leaves his boarding house in Oxford and goes to London to meet his new stepmother. When he sees her, he realizes that his father has married a vampire: "All of a sudden a smell, a smell, *that* smell." In occultist terminology a vampire was a pupa or an evil spirit given a new form, a larva or animal soul grown out of a person. Darío had followed closely the stories about Katie King whom the English occultist William Crookes had said was a dead woman among the living. He did not get carried away with morbidity, but structured his story skillfully with two points of view (his and Mr. Leen's), in two cities (Buenos Aires and London) and gave two solutions, madness or black magic.

Darío also made use of another kind of nightmare in his stories.

I cannot find words to describe the hypnagogic visions I so often have. They border on what might be called mathematical fantasies and are intimately associated with my preoccupations with the occult.

He goes on to give examples of nightmares in which an infinite number of fragments combine to form total images or, on the contrary, in which these images dissolve into thousands of geometrical figures like the decorative arabesques of oriental art. He surely was thinking of Poe when he called them "mathematical fantasies." In an article in *Los raros*, Darío associates imagination with madness, showing amazement at Poe's "mathematical momentum:"

. . . his fantasy is full of chimeras and ciphers like an astrologer's chart . . . The algebraic nature of his imagination produces melancholy effects when he takes us to the brink of the unknown.

He must have also been thinking of the "cabalistic Mallarmé," as Darío called him. In an essay published in *La Nación* (Buenos Aires), he attributed to Mallarmé the same characteristics the French poet had seen in William Beckford, author of *Vathek*,[15] a pseudo-oriental novel.

No one else could have so dedicated himself to the mathematical formulation of nightmarish effects: 'the melancholy produced by huge and monumental perspectives' . . . 'the dizziness (caused) by the oriental propensity for numbers.' Is it that we are overcome by a whirlwind of hypnological remembrances? For my part, I keep a fluttering memory of all such things as of a far-off world in which I once lived.

He could have possibly been thinking of Thomas De Quincey, whose *Confessions of an English Opium-Eater*, were familiar to him. Since these writings of Darío betray unconscious recollections of various authors, it is not surprising to find echoes of Poe, Mallarmé and De Quincey together on the same page.

In "La pesadilla de Honorio" (1894), Darío refers to De Quincey. Honorio remembers, without identifying it, the sentence: "that affection which I have called the tyranny of the human face"; and sees the face of the Malayan who visited De Quincey. Outside time and space, Honorio, alone and anguished, sees "in the distance the overwhelming, monumental perspective of strange architectures, visionary arrangements, styles of an unbridled, prodigious orientalism." (These words not only recall Beckford, Poe and Mallarmé, but also De Quincey's association of Piranesi's style of architecture with his own dreams: "with the same power of endless growth and self-reproduction did my architecture proceed in dreams . . . ; the splendours of my dreams were indeed chiefly architectural; dreams of oriental imagery . . . multiplied into ten thousand repetitions," etc.) Honorio foresees a universal cataclysm—the city disintegrates heralding the End of the World—then turns to watch a horrifying parade: "Before him had appeared the infinite legion of Faces and the innumerable army of Gestures. The images dissolve into an inferno of prisms and mirrors, finally becoming "the seven capital sins multiplied by seventy times seven." The story ends with the suggestion that this march of faces and masks entered the sleeping man's mind with the sounds of a carnaval that was passing through the street.

In "Cuento de Pascuas" (1911), the narrator, thanks to a drug, is able to perceive forms that ordinarily are invisible, but that he sees reproduce and change into others; the air, like a many-sided crystal, refracts light and a woman's head becomes the guillotined head of Marie Antoinette. In the frightening atmosphere of the French Revolution, under the light of a head-shaped moon, characters stumble on streets paved with heads, walk among trees whose fruits are heads, hear heads moaning . . . "And the heads multiply in groups, in gruesome heaps, in Paris, nerve center of the world."

One of Darío's best fantastic stories is "El caso de la señorita Amelia." In it, all the characters grow old with the exception of a twelve-year old girl. For her alone, time has stopped. Amelia, like Wendy who would be another Peter Pan, is the child who does not want to grow up. The difference is that James Barrie created a magical world while Darío—through his narrator Doctor Z, occultist, cabalist, student of oriental culture and black magic—presents an enigma that he believes will someday be solved by Theosophy. Incidentally this Doctor Z really lived. A few years later he appears in *Les Mystères de la Kabbale* by Eliphas Lévi. In Darío's story, Doctor Z corresponded with Madame H. P. Blavatsky, who in 1875 founded the Theosophic Society in New York. Before telling his story, the gnostic Doctor Z hesitates: he is afraid no one will believe him. Then Darío (or, at least, the first person narrator) encourages him with these words: " 'I believe,' I answered with a firm, calm voice, 'in God and in His Church. I believe in miracles. I believe in the supernatural.' " In this way Darío reconciled, as indeed he did in his own mind, Catholic theology and occultist theosophy.

Trusting in this religious syncretism, Darío believed in the reincarnation of the soul. This belief, one of whose first sources was Pythagoras, was his inspiration for many poems. It was less productive in his stories, in spite of the fact that Darío was familiar with excellent models. For one thing, he had read tales by Poe and Villiers de l'Isle Adam. Poe had treated the theme of reincarnation with glacial impartiality; Villiers de l'Isle Adam, an imitator of Poe, with transparent faith. As an unbeliever, Poe's stories were far superior, but Darío did not learn from his reading. Instead of writing stories of death with a free imagination, he let his knowledge of the occult sciences infect him. In poetry he intimated the theme of metempsychosis; in prose he hardly dared to. There was, however, one aspect of the belief in reincarnation that tempted him in his prose writings. He called it "euhemerism in reverse."

Euhemerus, who lived during the time of Alexander, had proposed the theory that gods and heroes were mythological figures derived from real men who had been benefactors of the people and, for that reason, had been turned into deities by posterity. According to Euhemerus, Zeus had once been a king of Crete, and Aphrodite a courtesan. In his essay, "Stéphane Mallarmé" (1898), Darío admires the idea of "earlier existences" and submits the theory of euhemerism in reverse, according to which it is possible to see incarnations of heroes in men today.[16] Much fantastic literature has been written around this theme; Darío even used it in some of his poems. He imagines that a certain friend had lived centuries before and that he, the poet, who had also had a previous existence, had known him then. The following example is from "Máximo Soto Hall," written in 1890, the year Darío was initiated into theosophy.

> I have seen you in a Florentine painting:
> You have been a sculptor, an artist, and a poet;
> . . . . .
> We have met somewhere along the way,
> And now, quite indiscreetly, I write about you.

José León Pagano ("Rubén Darío en mis recuerdos") cites an "Epístola" dedicated to Díaz Romero during Darío's years in Buenos Aires that begins:

> Pagano, being a pagan painter and a poet,
> Was in the Renaissance my friend and brother.
>
> During the Italian Renaissance I saw
> Someone who loved me and was just like you;
> . . . . .

> You looked proud, strong, overpowering, profound,
> As if you ruled the whole world.

It is not surprising that a poet should allude to magic in verse without rationalizing it. It is in prose, however, a medium used to express the writer's thought, to inform and to explain, where we can best see what was happening to Darío. He would think of a magical situation, but rather than tell it as pure invention, he preferred to substantiate it with occult science. The result was not a story, but an essay with a narrative structure. If he did come out with a story, it was burdened with elements that lacked any artistic form. When he was playing the occultist he was distracted and could not produce pure literature. Because he was too involved with his own beliefs and doubts, he did not elaborate some of his fantasies—the one of reincarnation, among others. *Tierras solares* is an example of how Darío simply failed to make the most of his material. He imagines a jump in time from the twentieth century to the sixteenth and a meeting with Blanco Fombona in Benvenuto Cellini's workshop.[17]

This morning, after reading some poems by R. Blanco Fombona, a fiery young poet, I had a strange feeling. It consisted of the following . . . :
Blanco Fombona is an old acquaintance of mine. I first met him at the home of the Cardinal of Ferrara, in Rome, where we were cordially introduced by *messer* Gabriel Cesano. Together we often visited the illustrious Benvenuto Cellini while he worked and later accompanied him during four days of escapades in Florence . . . We talked idly in the moonlight by the bans of the Arno . . . One night at an inn he beat a servant-boy. As a brawl ensued, he drew his sword and, when the constables were called in, I slipped away . . . Blanco Fombona was an avid supporter of the Medicis and was particularly fond of Lorenzo "the Magnificent" because he was a poet . . . Then he went to Flanders. In Paris he won the favor of King Francis. He quarrelled with the Primatrice because of Cellini and seriously wounded one of his worst enemies, an act for which he was put in prison . . . Being separated, I knew no more about him for a long time. A mutual friend from Rome told me he heard that he had gone to a far-off land, had taken part in a war, and had been made king. Another told me he had been killed. And still another that he had become a monk.

Behind all this there are the makings of a good story. Why didn't Darío write it? Here are his own reflections that round out the unsuccessful narration:

Today, on a hot morning of the May calends, in the year 1904, I have written, in the city of Florence, the preceding lines which I have since read several times carefully and reflectively. What do they represent: the product of imagination, the indelible recollection of a past existence, or the remainder of a dream? Let's go on to something else . . . A bit of cheap Alcanian wisdom wouldn't be bad, or some of the Hindu's and H.P.B.'s theosophy. Such means do not appeal to me. He who has eves should see. For the rest, all is useless!

This extra-literary observation is a symptom by which to diagnose what afflicted Darío at this time. The free flight of his imagination was deterred, he abandoned his theme, called on the credulity of others with like spiritual tendencies, and presented the "case" of his wanderings with Blanco Fombona through Benvenuto Cellini's Florence as something whose explanation could be found in the books of Felix Alban's library, in Hindu theosophy, or the writings of Madame H. P. Blavatsky.

When, on one occasion, the esoteric theme of pre-existence cedes to the theme of heroic madness, Darío, relieved from his fear of death, produces one of his best stories. The action takes place in the same year he had first spoken of euhemerism in reverse. The narrator relates an episode from his own experience during the Spanish American war. He describes a soldier he had seen in Santiago, Cuba: He was different from all the others; "he looked to be about fifty years old, but he might even have been three hundred. His sad gaze seemed to penetrate to the depth of our souls and tell us things of long ago." He is the standard bearer. He speaks very little, and then it is about dreams that could never come true. "He believes that shortly we will be in Washington and our flag will be flying over the Capitol." They all laugh at him: "They say that under his uniform he wears an old suit of armor." No one knows his name but his knapsack is stamped with two letters: D. Q. Suddenly the news is out: the Americans have won, "now Spain has nothing left of the world she discovered." They would have to surrender to the enemy.

When the time came to hand over the flag, something incredible happened that inspired awe in all those present. That strange man, whose eyes were as deep as the centuries, still carrying the red and yellow flag, gave us a look of bitter farewell and, as no one dared to touch him, slowly walked toward the cliff and jumped off. For what seemed a long time, we heard the sound of metal against rocks from the darkness of the precipice.

Then—euhemerism in reverse—everyone discovers in the soldier of 1898 none other than Don Quixote. The story is called "D. Q."[18]

Reality has been supplanted by an enigmatic and disturbing series of events with no more explanation than the one fantasy would provide. Darío wrote few fantastic stories of this type and quality. The lofty position he holds in literary history is due to his poetry, not to his fiction. But in a few cases he was also a master of the short story. Thus he was actually twice a master, the master-builder of an ivory tower as well as of a wind-swept tower of fantasy.

NOTES

[1] *Cuentos completos.* Edition and notes by E. Mejía Sánchez, Mexico, 1950. The fine study by Raimundo Lida that appears here as a prologue—"Los cuentos de Rubén Darío"—was revised, enlarged and published later in *Letras hispánicas,* Mexico, 1958.

[2] Two examples of verbal magic will suffice. In "La muerte de la emperatriz de la China", the situation is real. Darío took it from something a friend told him when he was in Chile. Pedro Balmaceda said he had fallen in love with a terra-cotta bust. Darío sets his story in Paris where two lovers quarrel because she, Suzette, is jealous of the affection Recaredo feels for the porcelain statue of a Chinese empress. In this woman's jealousy, no matter how contrived, we recognize very real human emotions. But Darío, through the use of poetic prose, gradually replaces this reality with an imaginary world. The story begins with a metaphor that strips Suzette of her human characteristics: she is a woman-jewel-bird who lives in a house-box-cage. The idealizing function of Darío's language is reinforced by a leitmotif of estheticism: the conflict between life and art. When Suzette, out of jealousy, breaks the porcelain bust, she repents and admits the superiority of art over life. Such anti-realism is even more evident in "Mi tía Rosa." The story is based on Darío's first encounter with love, an adolescent romance with his cousin whom he had mentioned in "Palomas blancas y garzas morenas" (*Azul*), and again in the fifth chapter of *La vida de Rubén Darío escrita por él mismo.* The evocation begins in the heavy style of a memoir. Suddenly it becomes a poem, ending with his aunt, transformed into a naked Venus, urging the youth to persevere in his love affair. If style is capable of changing real incidents like these, it seems valid to insist on its power to undo reality when from within historical circumstances it can suggest magical atmospheres—like in "Huitzilopoxtli"—or idylic atmospheres—"Historia de un 25 de mayo"—or when the very material for a story is fictitious—"El linchamiento de Puck." Often poetic style turns a story into a poem in prose: "Luz de luna," "Este es el cuento de la sonrisa de la Princesa Diamantina"; or the series of variations on the theme of the rose: "La resurrección de la rosa," "Preludio a Primavera," "El nacimiento de la col," "En la batalla de las flores." In the story "Por el Rhin" the delicate line of action is seen against the light inside a crystal ball and, there, is confused with multi-colored figures taken from *Faust* and other German sources. I might also add to what I have said the observations Raimundo Lida makes in his

study already cited, and what Rudolf Kochler says in "La actitud impresionista en los cuentos de Rubén Darío.", *Eco*, Bogotá, XIV, 84 (April 1967).

[3] Some of the designs of Darío's stories are very ingenious. If I had more time, and the means, I could diagram them with geometric or even topological clarity. In the place of diagrams, metaphors are handy. I would say, metaphorically, that there are some stories Darío decorated with the design of a fan, others with a pearl necklace, others with an hour glass. This is not the place to develop these metaphors either, but to demonstrate what I mean, I suggest that "Palimpsesto II" is an example of the hour glass design. We have to invert the story like we would an hour glass so that the action can continue. First position of the story-clock: a satyr and a centaur, although saddened by the death of the pagan gods, worship the God of the Christians. Second position: two hermits, Pablo and Antonio, announce that the satyr and the centaur will be rewarded for their conversion to the new faith. Think also of the pattern of a river that divides into two branches, and between islands and meanderings, finally disappears. In "Voz de lejos," the poet begins talking about the life of two saints, then his discourse breaks into fragments and falls apart. Or think of the design of a musical staff in "Las siete bastardas de Apolo," a verbal play on the names of notes and the double meaning of "sí" in the language of music and of women.

[4] A sequence that no sooner advances chronologically than it leaps back in time, then forward again. ("Voz de lejos").

[5] Narrative focuses according to the speaker's position outside of the story (perspectives of an omniscient author and of an observant author), or from within it (perspectives of the author-witness and the author-protagonist), with sudden changes when the point of view moves from that of the narrator to that of a character ("La pesca") or from one character to another ("Las razones de Ashavero").

[6] The story framed by words addressed to a friend which, in themselves, make up another story ("Un cuento para Jeanette"); the story with a "double" ("El Salomón negro"); the story that is interrupted when the narrator with deliberate irony begins to converse with an interlocutor or with the reader. In "Sor Filomela," for example, the author addresses himself to the reader: "And now, sir, I beg you to . . ." and an imaginary listener interrupts: "But doesn't what you're saying have to do with an actress?"

[7] Adaptions of hagiography ("La leyenda de San Martín, patrón de Buenos Aires"), apologues ("El nacimiento de la col"), theatrical dialogues ("Voz de lejos"), letters ("Carta del país azul"), memoirs ("Mi tía Rosa"), intimate diaries ("Esta era una reina"), allegories ("Cátedra y Tribuna"), etc.

[8] In "Un retrato de Watteau" from the series "En Chile" (*Azul*), it is suggested that an authentic marquise from the 18th century is making herself up in front of the mirrors in her rococo dressing room. In the end we find out that she is simply a woman from Santiago, Chile, getting ready for a masquerade ball. In "Por qué," there is a speech vibrant with moral indignation and revolutionary concern for justice. In the last lines of the story we learn that it has come from the mouth of a rogue. In his Epode II, Horace has the same kind of surprising twist. After an impressive description of the charms of rural life—"Beatus ille"—the speaker, Alfius, a money lender, returns to his anti-bucolic world. Using this same technique, Darío practically makes short stories of some of his chronicles. In *Todo al vuelo* there are pages where Darío describes the uneventful life of a run-of-the-mill

bureaucrat, then surprises us with the revelation that "he is the son of Paul Verlaine." The title of this selection is "El faunida"; that is, the son of the Faun, Verlaine.

9 Horace, *Odes*, William Hawthorn Mills, trans., (Lederer Street and Zeus Company: Berkeley (1921). [Translator's note.]

10 Fabio Fiallo, "El alma candorosa de Rubén Darío," *Rubén Darío y sus amigos dominicanos*. E. Rodríguez Demorizi (Bogotá, 1948).

11 S. T. Coleridge, *Biographia literaria*, II, 6, Cambridge, 1920.

12 "Onofroffismo. La comedia psíquica," *La Nación*, Buenos Aires, 1895, published in *Prosa dispersa*, Madrid, 1919. "Richard Le Gallienne," *Revista de América*, no. 2, 1894, included in *Obras completas*, vol. I, Madrid, Afrodisio Aguado, 1950–53. The information Darío had on spiritualism, esoteric sciences, demonology and theosophy is documented in "La Esfinge," a dialogue, yet to be published in book form, that appeared in *La Nación*, Buenos Aires, 16-III-1895 under the pseudonym "Misterium." In this dialogue, Alfa (who represents the skeptic side of Darío) converses with Omega (who represents his faith) about the magician Onofroff, a popular figure on the stage at that time in Buenos Aires.

13 A list of names associated with fantastic literature and cited by Darío should be compiled and should include not only men of letters but also "delvers in the occult" and pictorial artists who left some mark on his imagination. One should begin, of course, with *A Thousand and One Nights*, a literary archtype with oriental setting, and the authors of "terror" novels Darío read as a child, such as Jean Baptiste Regnault-Warin (*La caverne de Strozzi*, 1798) and the English novelists of the late 18th-century "Gothic revival." One should probably close with the authors of pseudo-scientific novels which fascinated Darío (see "El pueblo del polo," *Letras*, Paris, 1911). The following list, though incomplete, should prove useful. English and American: William Beckford, Max Beerbohm, Thomas DeQuincey, Arthur Conan Doyle, H. Rider Haggard, Lafcadio Hearn, Rudyard Kipling, Matthew Gregory Lewis, Edward Bulwer Lytton, Edgar Allan Poe, Ann Radcliffe, Robert Louis Stevenson, Horace Walpole, H. G. Wells, Oscar Wilde. French: Paul Adam, Honoré de Balzac, Léon Bloy, Edouard Dubus, Erckmann-Chatrian (Emile Erckmann and Alexandre Chatrian), Nicolas Camille Flammarion, Anatole France, Théophile Gautier, Théodore Hannon, Ernest Hello, Joris Karl Huysmans, Alfred Jarry, Lautréamont (Isidore Lucien Ducasse), Jean Lorrain (Paul Duval), Maurice Maeterlinck, Guy de Maupassant, Catulle Mendès, Prosper Merimée, Octave Mirbeau, Jean Moréas, Charles Nodier, Gérard de Nerval, Rachilde (Marguerite Eymery Vallette), Henri F. J. de Régnier, Jean Richepin, Marcel Schwob, Jules Verne, and Auguste Villiers de l'Isle Adam. Italian: Fra Domenico Cavalca and Antonio Fogazzaro. Spanish: Gustavo Adolfo Bécquer and Juan Valera. Delvers in the occult: Apuleius, Helena Petrovna Blavatsky, Jean Bodin, Jules Bois, Jacques Cazotte, William Crookes, Gérard A. V. Encausse ("Papus"), Joseph von Görres, Stanislas de Guaita, Eliphas Lévi, Paracelsus, Sar Josephin Péladan, Edouard Schuré, and Emanuel Swedenborg. Pictorial artists: Aubrey Beardsley, William Blake, Hieronymus Bosch, Peter Brueghel "the Elder," Paul Gauguin, Grandville (Jean I. Gérard), Charles de Groux, Victor Hugo (his drawings), Edvard Munch, Giambattista Piranesi, Odilon Redon, Félicien Rops, and J. M. W. Turner.

14 "Wells," in his *Obras Completas*. This was written after 1900.

[15] "Stéphane Mallarmé," *Escritos inéditos. Recogidos de periódicos de Buenos Aires y anotados por E. K. Mapes*, New York, 1938.

[16] *Ibid.*: "An euhemerism *à rebours*. Certain men living a temporary incarnation, having originally been gods, and presently maintaining a vague, clandestine relation with the Absolute. The suspicion or the certain knowledge of previous existences."

[17] The story of an encounter with Blanco Fombona and Benvenuto Cellini as Darío wrote it for *Todo al vuelo*, was published without the first lines, as "Prólogo para *Pequeña ópera lírica* de Rufino Blanco Fombona" (1904). On another occasion —"Primavera apolínea"—Darío again used fiction as the prologue to a book: a poet tells his life; he turns out to be Alejandro Sux, author of *La juventud intelectual de la América hispana*, (1911), the book Darío was introducing.

[18] "D.Q." appeared in Buenos Aires in the *Almanaque Péuser* around 1899. I thank E. H. Duffau for information on this date. Much later it was published in *Fray Mocho*, Buenos Aires, 13-I-1920. Ernesto Mejía Sánchez ("Un cuento desconocido de Rubén Darío," *Gaceta del Fondo de Cultura Económica*, México, XIII, 140, April 1966) took it from this source. Raimundo Lida tells me "D.Q." was reproduced in *Don Quijote*, Madrid, VIII, 8 (24-II-1899).

2

Sabia de la Sofía que sabe antiguas ciencias
Te asomas a veces entre imposibles muros,
Y más allá de todas las vulgares conciencias
Exploras los recodos más terribles y obscuros.

~~Y no encuentras~~

Y encuentras sombra y duelo. Que sombra y dolo encuentres
~~En la eterna enemiga que~~
Bajo la viña en donde nace el vino del Diablo.
Te posas en los senos, te posas en los vientres
Que hicieron a Juan loco e hicieron cuerdo a Pablo
A Juan virgen y a Pablo militar y violento.

[Fragment of Darío's autograph of *Divina Psiquis*]

BIBLIOGRAPHICAL NOTES
ON THE
CONTRIBUTORS

Enrique Anderson-Imbert is Victor S. Thomas Professor of Hispanic-American Literature at Harvard University. Among his works: *Estudios sobre escritores de América* (Buenos Aires: Editorial Raigal, 1954); *La crítica literaria contemporánea* (Buenos Aires: Gure, 1957); *El cuento español* (Buenos Aires: Columba, 1959); *Crítica interna* (Madrid: Taurus, 1961); *Los domingos del profesor* (México: Editorial Cultura, 1965); *El gato de Cheshire, narraciones* (Buenos Aires: Losada, 1965); *Spanish American Literature; a History;* translated from the Spanish by John V. Falconieri (Detroit: Wayne State University Press, 1963); *The Other Side of the Mirror* (*El grimorio*); authorized translation by Isabel Reade (Carbondale: Southern Illinois University, 1966). Professor Anderson-Imbert is the author of a study on Darío's poetry, included in the edition prepared by Ernesto Mejía Sánchez (Mexico: Fondo de Cultura Económica, 1952). "Los cuentos fantásticos de Rubén Darío" was published by Harvard University in May, 1967.

Miguel Enguídanos is Professor of Spanish and Portuguese at Indiana University. His works include that of associate editor of *Image of Spain* (with Ramón Martínez-López and Miguel González-Gerth), a special issue of *The Texas Quarterly* (June, 1961). Also: *La poesía de Luis Palés Matos* (Río Piedras: Ediciones de la Universidad de Puerto Rico, 1961). Profesor Enguídanos is the author of a study of Jorge Luis Borges included in the Argentine writer's *Dreamtigers*; translated by Mildred Boyer and Harold Morland (Austin: University of Texas Press, 1964). He is also currently preparing a book on the work of Darío. "Tensiones interiores en la obra de Rubén Darío" appeared in *Papeles de Son Armadans* (Madrid-Palma de Mallorca) nos. CXXXIII-VIII (agosto-setiembre de 1967).

Eugenio Florit is Professor of Spanish at Barnard College, Columbia University. He is co-editor of *Literatura hispanoamericana, antología e introducción histórica* (with Enrique Anderson-Imbert; New York: Holt, Rinehart and Winston, 1960). His authorship includes a study of José Martí's poetry included in Prof. Florit's edition of *Versos* (New York: Las Americas Publishing Co., 1962). Also many books of original poems including *Hábito de esperanza* (Madrid: Insula, 1965).

Allen W. Phillips was Professor of Spanish and Portuguese at Indiana University when this symposium took place; he is now at the University of Texas at Austin. His works include the following: *Ramón López Velarde, el poeta y el prosista* (México: Instituto Nacional de Bellas Artes, 1962), *Francisco González León, el poeta de Lagos* (México: Instituto Nacional de Bellas Artes, 1964), *Estudios y notas sobre literatura hispanoamericana* (México: Editorial Cultura, 1965). At present he is preparing a book on Ramón del Valle-Inclán.

Arturo Torres-Rioseco is Professor Emeritus of Latin American Literature at the University of California, Berkeley. He is the author of several works on Darío: *Rubén Darío, casticismo y americanismo; estudio precedido de una biografía del poeta* (Cambridge; Harvard University Press; London: Oxford University Press, 1931); *Vida y poesía de Rubén Darío* (Buenos Aires: Emecé Editores, 1944); *Antología poética de Rubén Darío* (selección, estudio preliminar, cronología, notas y glosario de Arturo Torres-Rioseco; Guatemala: Ediciones del Gobierno de Guatemala, 1948; Berkeley: University of California Press, 1949). Also: *Precursores del modernismo* (Madrid: Calpe, 1925; New York: Las Americas Publishing Co., 1963), *The Epic of Latin American Literature* (London: Oxford University Press, 1942; Berkeley: University of California Press, 1959), *Ensayos sobre literatura latinoamericana* (México: Tezontle; 1953; Berkeley, University of California Press, 1953), *Aspects of Spanish-American Literature* (Seattle: University of Washington Press, 1963).